HOW TO SURVIVE THE EMPTY NEST PHASE

PRACTICAL TIPS FOR EMPTY NESTERS TO RECONNECT WITH YOURSELF, YOUR ADULT CHILDREN, AND SPOUSE WHILE REIGNITING YOUR INNER PURPOSE

PAMELA FARIOLE

D1738446

COPYRIGHT

�֎ Created with Vellum

TABLE OF CONTENTS

INTRODUCTION

Do you believe in miracles? If I were to ask you what meaning they hold to you, or if you have ever experienced one, you would simply think about your children.

There is no relationship as selfless as a parent-child one. You commit to a lifetime of experiencing overwhelming emotions the minute you conceive your child. From carrying them inside your womb to changing their diapers, crying when they cry, laughing when they laugh, and feeling their emotions like your own, they become a part of you, and you become a part of them. It is inevitable. Your life has been centered on their schoolwork, social activities, and carpooling for at least 18 years, while your children recognize you as their sole pillar of strength.

Every morning, you have woken up to the thought

of their well-being, preparing their breakfast, providing them lunch for school, looking after their nutritional needs, and nurturing them with all the love you hold in that heart of yours. It seems like only yesterday they were bringing home toads and turtles or smiling with pride as they wheeled the book cart through the school premises. Indeed, no emotions compare to the ones you feel when you realize, from changing their diapers to witnessing their high school graduation, your little one has grown up and is ready to leave for college.

Although your dream has always been to see your children as healthy, independent young adults, embracing this change can be difficult and occasionally even painful, causing you to suffer from empty nest syndrome. The agony of separation may be far worse than merely missing your child once they have moved out. You might experience a very profound sense of loss and sadness, as well as a lack of control or direction. Don't worry! No matter how bad it feels right now, your feelings are absolutely justified.

The responsibilities of the role you have successfully been fulfilling every day may now shift considerably. As a parent, you are used to getting things done your way. But now, they seem to be slipping out of your hands, and you might not be as big of a part of your child's life as you have been previously.

Not only that, you might be undergoing an identity crisis, especially if your identity has always been heavily entwined with raising your children. Having previously identified as a "soccer mom" or a "stay-at-home dad, " you may question your identity or place in society. This is especially true for women since they are frequently trained to value themselves based on their ability to take care of others and to prioritize others' needs over their own. They alter their educational or job paths when children are born; as a result, when their children leave the nest, they feel a profound loss of connection and purpose.

Additionally, the biggest challenge for you may be overcoming the feeling that you are no longer required in your child's life while simultaneously feeling "ancient," knowing you have raised your kids to maturity and have fulfilled the ultimate objective of your life.

The sadness of empty nest syndrome often goes unrecognized since an adult kid moving out of home is perceived as a regular, healthy event, unlike the loss experienced when a loved one passes away. There may not be many people who can empathize or assist upset parents, although the transition can put you through an overpowering sense of bereavement.

I remember my heart sinking to my stomach and my throat clenching when my oldest left for college subsequently, my son and youngest daughter followed suit and eventually left home, sought new careers scattered across the country. In complete loneliness, I had prepared for the day in advance, over and over again. I did not want my children to see their pillar of strength displaying signs of weakness. Despite all my preparations, my plans came crashing down as soon as I saw my youngest daughter driving away from me. The magnitude of my feelings of uncertainty and sorrow knocked me down pretty badly.

So, the real question is, what do us grieving parents do now?

The time of adjustment after your child has been sent off to college is crucial. The path you choose to take during this period determines how you will cope with this change.

Reconnecting with yourself is the first step toward recovery. Ask yourself, "What would you do if you had to devote the same amount of effort to caring for yourself as you would for a child?" What would make you happier or more fulfilled? Whom would you like to spend your time with? It is probably challenging for you to answer these questions, but don't be upset. Keep in mind that for approximately eighteen years, your attention has been frequently directed away from yourself toward your child or children. To focus that attention back on yourself can be difficult. The overwhelm you are experiencing can hinder your thought process, but with the right help and guidance, there is nothing you cannot overcome.

A little shift in perspective, some self-care, newfound goals, and a reconnection with your loved ones can easily take you through the three steps that outline empty nesting; grief, relief, and joy.

One of the most challenging times in my life began when I underwent the empty nester's syndrome, but it was also then that I learned a lot about myself. I never knew I had the ability and the strength to endure those challenges alone. While it is true that having someone to help you through the journey makes it easier, the long-term benefits come when you learn to deal with it all yourself. That's when you realize your true resilience.

Having experienced all these feelings before you, I wrote this book to assist you in discovering the precise tactics you need to pick yourself up and resume living your life where you left it before becoming a parent. Undoubtedly, parenthood teaches you a lot, be it when you are living with your children or without. While you have so beautifully raised them and learned so much in the process, it is now time for you to learn more being by yourself.

To get me through my grief, I took solace in the fact that I will always be a parent to my three children, even if it is not precisely the way I am used to. The same goes for you, too. That's a promise.

So, let's dive right into the chapters and get into the details of what you are here for; the strategies to surviving the agony of having your children leave the house and flourishing and finding happiness in our daily lives.

CHAPTER 1: WHAT JUST HIT ME?

"Sometimes love means letting go when you want to hold on tighter." —Melissa Marr

I still remember the first few minutes of stillness and empty silence when I returned home after my last child left home. The way back home felt like the longest drive of my life, with this hollowness in my heart traveling up to my throat, clenching it fully. My thoughts began racing; it felt like my life was almost ending or at the very least the familiar life I lived certainly was ending. How am I supposed to accept that I won't see my child/children every day anymore? The same faces I started my day and completed my night with for 18 years. Does the universe expect me to be okay with this? Inside my head, one question after the other popped, but I had no answer to any of them. And that made it all so much worse. Is anything worse than being in an overwhelming situation and not knowing what to do? I believe not.

In today's world, we all rely on the internet to answer questions we don't seem to have answers to. And that's what I did. I searched for my condition in hopes of finding some source of solace. The empty nest syndrome; that's what I was suffering from. It was good to know the condition had a name; it provided me with validation for how I felt. It must be commonly experienced, right?

For those of you who may not know, empty nest syndrome is not a disease or an illness. Instead, it is a condition characterized by parents (usually the primary caretaker) feeling upset and alone after their children leave the nest to pursue studies at a college or university (mostly). As parents, the thought of our children graduating can make us quite excited since we believe it to be a significant event for them and us, but it comes along with the need to make a great transition. We have no choice but to stay home without engaging in our kids' usual activities, living a life without any individuals requiring our care, and being lonely in the nest that was once full of life. This change dramatically impacts many parents who find the adjustment to be challenging. The critical point is that it may develop into extremely serious depression, anxiety, lack of purpose, or other problems, even if you may just feel a tiny bit of sadness or loneliness that people may think is normal. Additionally, the extrinsic factors in your life may also be troubling you simultaneously, which could affect the duration you experience the Empty Nest Syndrome. Still, usually, it lasts around two months but can last up to 2 years, depending upon additional factors.

E very individual is unique; we go through varying experiences, live in dissimilar environments, are born with distinct genetics, and have different learning capabilities and personalities. All these things shape how we endure the hardships that life throws our way (Morin, 2020). While some people are born mentally strong, others train their minds to become that way. It doesn't make us any better or worse than each other, but it simply outlines our thought processes which impact our ability to cope with big or small changes in life.

S o, looking inside yourself is essential in understanding why you feel the way you do. Analyzing your circumstances to determine the potential causes of why you feel as awful as you do is a great way to begin this introspection. Here's a list of things that could be deciding your feelings:

Resistance to change

Do you resist change? Change can be intimidating. It expects us to break out of the patterns we have been following for so long. Because we are so familiar with these old patterns, we feel a lot more in control when working alongside them. But when we are required to change them, things begin feeling out of control. That loss of direction may be what we resist. Even the simplest things in unkept routines can rock my world such as the thought of leaving the house with my bed unmade, pj's in a ball on the floor as well as coffee cup stains and toast crumbs left on the counter will start my day off badly. I personally do not like change and this empty, quiet home was a very difficult transition for me. The silence was deafening.

Past experiences

Did you have difficulty moving out from your own home? Our childhood experiences shape who we are. When these experiences haven't been too pleasant for us to remember, going through something similar can cause a lot of distress, also known as post-traumatic stress disorder when the distress is extreme.

Your marital/relationship status.

What is the status of your marriage? Is your marriage in rough shape/unstable? Are you married to a stranger now? Have you both been going separate ways for years? Are you recently divorced, separated, going through a breakup, single for a long time, or married, but the marriage may need to be salvaged with work and help? Are you staying in a marriage for the kids sake because knowing the devil you are with is better than the unknown?

Many couples put their romance on hold to focus solely on raising their children. After the kids are grown and gone, your marriage may need some repair if you've unintentionally or intentionally neglected it for years. If all of your activities as a couple centered on the school and activities of your children, you might not know what to do with yourselves. The process of reestablishing contact might be a little complex. Additionally, some couples discover that their responses to having empty nests vary. I have girlfriends who were doing the "let's go to Disney" chant like the commercial seen on tv years ago. For me, that would be the last place I would want to go. The thought of being surrounded by families and kids would be like rubbing salt in my wounds. The relationship may be tenser if one of you is coping better or enjoying life without children in the home more than the other.

Many partners also may unfortunately undergo physical or mental abuse at the hands of the other. The constant digs, cut downs, snide remarks, jokes at your expense, the silent treatment and the like add a coolness and distance that can become a pattern of familiar. This can add to the emotional turmoil they are already suffering, thus making them more prone to the depression and anxiety felt during the empty nest syndrome.

On the other hand, for single parents, the loneliness

of not having a partner to share the pain with can be challenging if you are separated. The lack of a partner can make the house feel even more empty.

Financial situation

Do you have financial instability? Do your finances, in turn, offer no security due to the unknown? Are you clueless about the finances? Did you let your spouse handle all of that? Are you totally dependent on your spouse? Do you feel like your protected cocoon has been torn apart and shattered, and now you are vulnerable to God knows what?

This is a time when you are already experiencing uncertainty and vulnerability in your life. Any other factor that adds more of that could be worsening the situation for you. Everyone longs for a soft landing and financial security however as in all situations the degree of security depends on decisions made years ago and how well you were able to plan and save for times such as these. Maybe you and your spouse have different money languages and you need to reign in and get aligned with each other towards a common goal.

Past child-rearing experiences

As mentioned earlier, we all differ in many ways. For some parents, it may have always been harder to lose that connection with their kids that they are used to having. This can stem from several reasons, such as a loss of control or the fear that your child may not be as much yours as they were before.

Ask yourself, was it hard to let go during your children's milestones? Were you devastated when each child left for first grade, kindergarten, and daycare all the way up to college? Was it difficult to wean your baby from breastfeeding?

If the majority of answers are "yes," that can help you understand why you feel this way.

Identity crisis

Do you know who you are? Stay-at-home moms may lose their identity as their roles become their self-identity versus people with a strong sense of self-worth. Have you lost your way and have difficulty remembering the person you were before your kids? Do you hear yourself introducing yourself as so and so's mom rather than who you are? Full-time stay-at-home moms are affected more than people with other responsibilities, such as employment outside the home. Have your children's lives become yours? Do you have little preparation for job skills as your role was the caretaker and housekeeper?

Single parents or marriages with absentee dads may also be more susceptible to this identity crisis, as they give much of themselves to their kids. They are frequently required to do everything on their own, compared to parents who are married or cohabiting, and may be able to squeeze in a few hours of free time each week or sleep a little later because of the assistance of another parent. This results in less sleep, less free time, and less time for other activities for a single caretaker. To fulfill their responsibility toward their kids, they forgo professional changes, romantic relationships, new interests, and friendships, ultimately being left with no identity of their own.

After the kids leave the nest, mothers who have no professional life may feel worthless because their primary source of self-fulfillment is missing now. And even when they decide to resume their professional lives, they may find themselves lacking the skills the corporate world expects them to have. This can worsen their identity crisis.

Depression and Anxiety

Do you feel anxious wondering if you prepared your child enough to take on the world alone? Do you feel grief as you will no longer know what is happening in their lives? Can you no longer control situations or protect them from harm? Are you the mama bear whose role has been shattered, who feels no longer needed, disoriented, and pushed aside? That was me for awhile. I truly felt lost and wondered what brought me joy before kids? I certainly must have had a life and felt happy and fulfilled but could honestly not think of anything that topped being a parent.

A major reason behind anxiety disorders originates from the fear of the unknown (Parmet, 2016). Not knowing what is to come can be terrifying when you have previously always known what to expect from your daily life at home with your kid(s). Moreover, it can be upsetting to suddenly lose control of your children's life. While these fears and anxious thoughts are not abnormal, they can turn into dangerous disorders if they persist for too long (Bailey, 2008).

Additionally, people who already experience anxiety have a much higher chance of acquiring depression (Tjornehoj, n.d.). This depression can cause further anxiety, creating an endless cycle. Staying in this state is debilitating and no way to live. Information regarding treatment suggestions will come later in this book.

Midlife crisis

A midlife crisis is characterized as a period of emotional upheaval between the ages of 40 and 60 that is accompanied by an intense yearning for change. Middle age can offer distinct life transitions, such as your children leaving your nest, unlike earlier and later periods of life, even if adjusting to change is an unavoidable aspect of the human experience.

Because you have been so focused on your children and their needs, when that dynamic changes, you start looking more at yourself, analyzing every minor and major change in your now unusual life. Both males and females tend to feel dissatisfied with their own personal achievements thus far in life regretting decisions or lack of decisions made. You might discover your job path is less than acceptable and regret not pursuing employment you deem more meaningful; you might start to recognize your physical skills have diminished with age, your relationships are not what fulfills you; or you might realize you missed a significant objective you intended to achieve along the way (Simon, 2022). This may make you feel unachieved and worthless, thus compounding an empty nester's grief. The various challenges and upheavals during this phase in life seem immense but tackling one at a time is how you win the battles.

Menopause

It is a syndrome in which the levels of circulating sex hormones fall for both genders. The sex hormone in women will drop suddenly, whereas it will gradually drop in men.

30% of men in their 50s will likely have some andropause symptoms, which are brought on by decreasing testosterone levels (Ubaidi, 2017).

These dropping hormones also cause a decrease in serotonin levels, a brain chemical that fosters positive emotions, ultimately leading to an increase in irritation, anxiety, and sorrow (Payne, n.d.). Hot flashes, decreased sex drives and irritability all add up to being a hot mess however this too shall pass.

How to handle depression and stress?

While the unwavering emotions of grief and stress you are undergoing might feel endless, remember that every cloud has a silver lining, and no time is permanent, be it happy or sad.

Here are a few coping mechanisms you can apply (*Empty Nest Syndrome*, n.d.):

- Recognize your grief and permit yourself to be upset. Even if others don't seem to understand your situation, don't let their invalidation define what you feel.

- Different rituals, like funerals, help people get closure. Make up your own rituals to assist you in recognizing your emotions. You may consider rearranging your child's former room or planting a tree.
- Talk to your partner about your ideas, emotions, and hopes for the future. This can help bring you two on the same page and give more direction to your life.
- Seek counsel and comfort from other friends who share your feelings; some of them may have also dealt with empty nest syndrome. Not only will they validate your feelings, but you may also be able to get advice from someone who has been through it before.
- Spend some time getting used to the changes. Don't set yourself up for failure by setting high expectations for yourself, especially in the early weeks or months. If you become too hard on yourself, you are likely to face disappointments when you cannot act as you planned in your head. Take one day at a time, don't rush the process.
- Await your feeling of adaptation before making any significant decisions. Before you plan to introduce newer and greater changes to your life, such as shifting to a new house, allow yourself to first cope with not having your children around anymore. We often make emotional decisions that we believe will

help us in the future, but we regret them later because of their impracticality that we forgot to recognize earlier.

- Utilize the extra time you have to pursue your interests and hobbies. Before having your children, you may have had dreams to fulfill that you sacrificed for them. Rekindle those passions in you. If you feel like you have changed as a person, figure out what you like doing now. While some think creative expression is beneficial, others get calm in prayer. Act in a way that seems right to you.

- Maintain consistent habits and self-care practices, such as eating a balanced diet and exercising frequently. They will help you better your physical, mental, and emotional health and well-being while encouraging favorable health outcomes, like building resilience, longer life expectancy, and better stress management skills (Lawler & Laube, n.d.). Start small, even if you walk to the end of your street and back at least that is progress. Eventually walk the neighborhood and keep expanding from there.

- If you are feeling overwhelmed, get expert assistance. If stress lingers on for too long, it can cause physical ailments like heart disease (*Stress*, n.d.). Get professional help as soon as you can if stress develops into a serious condition. Severe depression might result from untreated anxiety problems (Sawchuk, n.d.).

By now, you must have understood what happened to you is not unusual. The emotions you feel are absolutely warranted, but staying the same way and doing nothing about your situation is not a good idea. The point is for you to try to sort out the difficult, unwelcome position of being in the middle of the empty nest stage of life. If you require assistance to get through this initial stage of despair and mourning the familiar existence that is no longer there, don't hesitate. After all, nobody can change your days only you can create the change you want to see in yourself. How can you get this help? Let's talk about that now.

CHAPTER 2: CRY YOURSELF A RIVER; JUST DON'T DROWN

"You will never achieve what you are capable of if you are too attached to the things you need to let go of." —Unknown

Do your mornings begin with you trying to depuff your eyes? The crying from last night, the night before that, and the night before that, and the night before (you get the point) can leave you with eye bags, a swollen face, and a stuffy nose. Do you walk around in a zombie state? Your life seems to be falling apart, and your body is in no mood to cooperate, either.

I remember when I was going through my empty nest phase. I cried enough tears at one point, so I bought a kayak. Okay, no, just kidding. But I swear the idea crossed my mind a few times.

God provided us with our kids for a while, and now the time for raising them has passed. We grew them to be able to fly and have wings; our job is done now, but shouldn't we be happy? Everybody has a special way of sifting through the confusion of conflicting ideas and feelings. It's acceptable to lament the loss and worry about unwelcome developments, but staying like that is not okay. Grieving is a process of healing. You're concluding that chapter of your life and lamenting the additions your children made to the days that were previously filled with an excess of unfathomable delight. There has been a great loss, and your depression is quite genuine. But you can't be stuck in this sad state forever, right?

There are abundant ways to come out of this. What you choose depends on what you feel comfortable with. However, remember that sometimes it is important to break out of your comfort zone to change your days. Let's look at some of these ways.

Natural Remedies to Decrease Depression and Anxiety

Medicines can be intimidating for many people.

Some of us have had bad experiences with conventional treatments, while others may like to stay away from chemicals and prefer natural remedies to fight their physical and psychological issues. I personally like to try out herbal medicines or solutions before I make a move to conventional ones. If the job gets done naturally, there's nothing better for me.

The good news is that there are many natural ways to battle depression. I have tried a few myself.

Saffron

The symptoms of depression may be exacerbated by anxiety, stress, and low mood. Natural items like saffron, which have been found promising after showing positive effects on major depressive illnesses, constitute a pertinent option among non-pharmacological ways to improve subclinical mood symptoms and resilience to stress (Jackson et al., 2021).

Like other antidepressants, saffron may work to alleviate depression by adjusting the quantities of specific neurotransmitters in the brain, such as serotonin (a mood-elevating neurotransmitter) (Hausenblas et al., 2013).

For mild to moderate depression, use 20 to 30 mg/day of saffron extract (petal or stigma) (*Saffron Uses, Benefits & Dosage*, 2022).

. . .

St Johns Wort

St. John's wort is a flowering shrub that is indigenous to Europe. It is sold as a dietary supplement widely used to treat depression and menopausal symptoms (Mayo Clinic, n.d.). According to numerous research, the supplement has been shown to be effective in treating mild to moderate depression (Mayo Clinic, n.d.). In fact, several studies have revealed that the supplement is just as effective as many antidepressants prescribed by a doctor (Mayo Clinic, n.d.). It works by enhancing the activity of brain chemicals like noradrenaline and serotonin, which are believed to be crucial in mood regulation (*What Is St John's Wort?*, 2022).

Vitamin D and Omega 3 Fatty Acids

Every functioning activity that regulates our body's system depends on the availability of a range of nutrients in sufficient amounts. An adequate supply of nutrients ensures each function is carried out in the best way possible to support health. Looking after our children all the time, we forget to provide our bodies with the bare necessities it needs to thrive. Hence, adults frequently have vitamin D deficiencies and insufficiencies, and most also don't get enough omega-3 fatty acids. Both of these have significant impacts and benefits on the health of the brain and neurological system, thus improving depression, stress, anxiety, and sleep (*Combining Vitamin D and Omega-3s Produced the Greatest Improvements for Depression, Anxiety and Sleep,* 2021).

Regular Exercise

Exercising frequently might feel like the last thing you want to do while you're undergoing sadness or anxiety. However, exercise can significantly impact your mental health by releasing feel-good endorphins, endogenous cannabinoids, and other naturally occurring brain chemicals that can improve your sense of well-being and put worries aside to break the cycle of pessimistic thinking that feeds depression and anxiety (Mayo Clinic, n.d.).

Additionally, it may make you feel more 'achieved' when you meet the exercise goals you set for yourself and choose a healthy path as your coping mechanism rather than indulging in alcohol, chocolate or sulking in sadness.

Get Adequate Sleep

Have you ever had people asking you if you woke up on the wrong side of the bed after you woke up feeling all grumpy? That phrase came into existence for a reason.

Sleep is directly linked to mental and emotional well-being and has been associated with conditions like bipolar disorder, anxiety, and depression, among others. The brain's ability to interpret emotional information is facilitated by getting enough sleep. It analyzes and retains thoughts and memories when we sleep. A lack of sleep is particularly detrimental to consolidating emotionally positive information. Without positive things to remember, you are bound to focus on the negative ones, which can lead to suicidal thoughts or actions and affect mood and emotional reactivity (Suni, 2022). Put yourself in time-out and get some well needed rest.

Join Support Groups for Empty Nesters

You may feel like nobody understands you or what you are going through. However, joining a support group gives you a chance to interact with individuals who are likely to share a common goal and comprehend one another. Because of their shared experiences, support group participants frequently have comparable thoughts, anxieties, practical issues, treatment choices, and adverse consequences (Mayo Clinic, 2022). As a result, you may (Mayo Clinic, 2022):

- feel less judged, lonely, or alone
- experience lower levels of anxiety, weariness, despair, or distress
- feel free to express expressing your emotions honestly
- enhance your coping mechanisms for obstacles in your way.

If you are not willing to go out and interact with people physically, you can also join Facebook groups for empty nesters.

Workbook to Help

Mind Over Mood: Change How You Feel By Changing the Way You Think by Dennis Greenberger, Christine Padesky. Aaron T Beck

This amazing workbook teaches readers how to use cognitive therapy to enhance their lives. It includes worksheets that walk you through each stage and teach precise techniques that have helped countless individuals overcome issues such as depression, anxiety attacks, panic attacks, rage, guilt, shame, low self-esteem, eating disorders, substance misuse, and marital issues. Readers learn how to utilize mood questionnaires to recognize, evaluate, and monitor changes in feelings, alter problematic beliefs, apply step-by-step techniques to elevate moods, and take action to enhance daily activities and interpersonal interactions.

Talk to Family and Friends

Talking your feelings out with your loved ones can offer you the comfort you may be looking for. It can reduce your feelings of loneliness and bring you the reassurance you may need. According to (Griffiths et al., 2011), family and friends are well placed to provide the support that receivers perceive to be positive, which can assist them in obtaining formal mental health treatment if and when needed. You may also find some loved ones who have been through this phase before. They can guide you well and give you important tips that may have worked for them. Sitting around a campfire with a glass of wine, and a friend can be just the right medicine for your weary soul.

Join a Women's Bible Study Group

The Bible is full of examples of people who have endured great hardships and found their way through changing circumstances. Joining a women's Bible study group can help ease your grief religiously. The verses from the Bible are discussed and used as a guiding light to navigate through significant transitions in your life. Read the chapters entitled loneliness, depression, courage, emotions, fear, forgiveness, help, hope, anxiety, and worry, they have scriptures verses to read and meditate on daily. Here are a few examples of verses you may find helpful:

- God is my shield and the lifter of my head. - Psalm 3.3
- God is my refuge and strength, an ever-present help in trouble. Psalm 46:1 (NIV)
- I cast the whole of my care (all my anxieties, all my worries, all my concerns, once and for all on Him, for He cares for me affectionately and cares about me watchfully. -1Peter5:7

- I am confident of this very thing, that He who has begun a good work in me will complete it until the day of Jesus Christ. Philippines 1:6 (NKJV)

While these natural ways of coping with depression and anxiety can prove to be successful for many, that is not always the case. Give these strategies a try, but if they don't work for you, make sure to seek professional help. I remember as I sat numb and depressed in my lawn chair, I heard voices nearby that sounded like my daughter and her boyfriend. I instantly sprung up from my trance with excitement thinking they were home for dinner. However, when I realized it was the voice of the neighbor's teenage son and his friend, it jolted me back to reality and made me realize I was alone. To make matters worse, the ice cream truck came down the block while playing that carnival music, bringing back painful memories of my kids begging for quarters so they could buy ninja turtles ice cream pops and rainbow popsicles. As the floodgates opened and tears gushed out, I realized I needed assistance from the outside world. It is acceptable to receive temporary antidepressants and seek expert counseling if need be. Stigmas around mental health can discourage you from seeking help, but staying in this horrible state forever is much worse than fighting those stigmas. Not only will you actually be able to do something about your condition, but you will also feel good about yourself after breaking these toxic stereotypes. Plus, it always helps to talk your feelings out with someone who can understand, validate and help you navigate through them, doesn't it?

CHAPTER 3: THE GOOD, THE BAD & THE UGLY

"Not until we are lost do we begin to find ourselves."—Henry David Thorea

So now, you know several ways to reduce your depression and anxiety. But what about those worries that keep you up at night, the troubled thoughts that shoot your anxiety and keep you from functioning properly through the day? The thoughts of your house being an empty chilly bunch of wood and nails compared to the home it was once. While over-the-counter medication, temporary prescribed medication, and strategies can help ease the pain for you, they can never solve the problem. The only way to tackle them is to understand their origin. It is necessary to eliminate each reason for worry one by one, but that cannot happen unless you figure out what each reason is.

I t is time to create a plan to reduce your discomfort after assessing and evaluating where it is coming from. You may be worried about how you will fit into your child's life, if your loneliness is here to stay, what your child/children must be doing without you, who you can talk to in your grief-stricken state, how you will manage your finances, will you be okay; the list may seem endless. Start with what you can manage and take incremental moves. Work through your list of obstacles one at a time, ranking them in order of severity from the most upsetting to the least. It is an opportunity for social, physical, emotional, and spiritual reflection. You must set priorities and work through each obstacle one at a time, even though the list looks never-ending and daunting. Since everyone does not face the same obstacles, everyone will have distinct lists. Some parents are less affected since they are ready for this stage of life in advance, but others are completely unprepared and carried away.

T ake a deep breath. Although life might seem the most challenging it has ever been, you are more resilient than you might realize.

. . .

L et's look at empty nesters' most commonly faced problems and figure out ways to tackle them.

L oss of self
Ask yourself, what do you define yourself as? If the answer has something to do with your children, of course, you will feel like you have lost yourself after they leave your nest. It's normal to experience this sort of grief as you adjust and come to grips with the realization that a part of your life has come to an end. However, you can discover new meaning in your life after you use your free time to start a new activity or take on a challenging task. Just keep in mind that a new chapter is starting in both your child's and your own lives, and it is not the end of anything but the beginning of better things.

The guilt of past parenting and not being more available to them

As a parent, you must be very familiar with the feelings of guilt gushing all over you. Everything made you feel guilty, from being looked at as an irresponsible parent for buying your toddler candies at the supermarket to the expression in your toddler's eyes when you lost your cool after they left their bed for the tenth time. But now that you have all the time in the world to overthink how you may have somehow wronged your children once, maybe a harsh word spoken in anger you regret saying, the guilt can hit you differently. You can't really work on and improve your parenting skills anymore since you have no children left at home. The good news is, you don't need to either. All this guilt comes from your overthinking. In reality, you probably have been a better parent than you believe. If you feel a need to apologize to you children do so and make peace with yourself. No one is given a book on how to be the perfect parent. Forgive yourself for being human.

Think of it like this, do you remember when you were a child, other kids cycled around the streets while their parents were at work? And when your parents were younger, it was common for their parents to light a cigarette while putting a newborn to sleep. And before that, elder siblings parented younger ones while the parents made ends meet. Am I saying that's the right way to parent? What I am saying is every parent does the best they can with how equipped or prepared they were to being parents and we cannot beat ourselves up.

Concern for your children

Worrying about your children's well-being once they have moved out of the house is okay. However, constantly worrying about how your child is doing is not normal. Don't make them feel suffocated by constantly checking up on them, asking them if they have been eating well, getting enough sleep, feeling safe, need help with assignments, etc. We have all seen the negative affects of helicopter moms and how that hovering affects kid's self esteem.

Every healthy relationship occasionally needs some

space. This space is not just important for your child to explore their individuality and their abilities to grow without your help, but also for you to understand yourself and focus more intently on your feelings. By allowing yourself time to reflect and work through your feelings, you lessen your tendency to snap at your partner or use poor communication techniques (*How to Create Space in Your Relationship*, 2020). Overall, having space offers emotional clarity, the chance to attend to our particular needs, and a sense of individuality we can all use.

In the end, trust yourself and what you have taught your children through these 18 years to be enough for them. Overlook their messy apartments or dorm rooms with scattered empty beer bottles, dirty dishes in the sink, and discarded microwave meals in the trash. Let them figure out their lives while you figure things out for yourself.

Nervous about being in an unstable marriage

Remember when you first had your children, you felt upset about not getting enough time to spend with your partner? Longing for a date night, and planning who might be available to come babysit for an hour or two. Then having limited time away together just became the norm, and you both adapted to the circumstances, shifting your focus from one another to bringing up your kids together and sometimes separately.

But now that the kids are gone, you have all the time to spend with each other. However, it doesn't feel the same because what was once the norm changed and is now asking to be the norm again?! Instead of cribbing over this, consider this time a chance to get back in touch with your spouse and remember what first made you fall in love. To avoid becoming a grumpy old woman snapping at a grumpy old man, focus on the positive rather than all the little annoying habits your spouse does and vice versa. Allowing each to share a small part in each others' lives may seem awkward at first but then a welcomed change. For example, take your wife out in that awesome golf cart of yours and show her how the game is played. Maybe you can take hubby out for a couples' massage and then a nice lunch. More suggestions to come on things you can do together to reconnect.

Concerns about your financial situation

Even if your home is empty, you may be spending more than ever due to the high expense of higher education. This could really make you worried about your own personal financial situation.

Nearly 52% of parents said that helping their children pay for college was more crucial than saving for their own retirement (Stern, 2015). Similarly, 53% of participants stated they would prefer to withdraw funds from their retirement account if doing so would prevent their kids from having to take out student loans (Stern, 2015).

You may not have assessed how much of your budget could be spent on your children's college fees. You may have also "maxed-out" your ability to obtain loans to get your children enrolled in college. Whatever the reason, it is time to review your financial situation and bring yourself out of it. How can you do that? More on that in a while. A chapter is devoted on debt reduction for those who this applies.

Practical tips for empty nesters

Some parents start preparing for their children's day of departure early on. But that's not how it is for everyone. Outlined by Strategies for Overcoming Empty Nest Syndrome (n.d.), here are some strategies to help overcome the empty nest syndrome.

List the roles you play

Roles such as those of a sister, wife, husband, brother, neighbor, pet parent, cook, or employee often define who we are. Identify which of the responsibilities on your list you might be able to extend as you go through it. For instance, if you're married or have a partner, you could recommit to the union, discover fresh common interests, and reignite your romance. You might think about going out on dates again if you are single. You can consider building a better relationship with your neighbor, enhancing your cooking skills, or stepping up for community involvement.

Respect the timing

Do not evaluate your child's schedule compared to your own experiences or expectations. Instead, concentrate on what you can do to support your child's success once they leave home. If you give off the impression that you will crumble once they leave, they won't be able to withdraw emotionally, which is crucial for their growth. Unintentionally burdening our children with our own issues is not fair. For example, in the beginning stages of the empty nest, my children would call to check in on me. I did not want them to carry my sadness as their burden and that is when I got busy working on me. Of course, our children will always be our child(ren), but we now need to develop a more mature, independent adult bond with them.

Maintain contact

Even if you don't live together, you can stay close to your kids. Today, staying in touch with your kids is much simpler because of mobile phones and the internet. Try to keep in touch regularly via visits, calls, emails, messages, and video chats. Discuss a reasonable expectation for the frequency of contact with your child. Encourage your other siblings to maintain contact with your college-bound children. I found zoom calls were great as I could chat looking at his/her face while chatting, feeling that closeness, and having the reassurance that he/she is happy and well.

Get your child(ren) ready

If it's not too late, and your child still has time before they leave, prepare them for the change to come. Both you and your child will benefit from it. By doing this, you can stop worrying about whether they can prepare a meal, wash their own laundry, stick to a budget or manage a check book. Make sure you have taught them the fundamentals because if they are not prepared, they will continue to depend on you, which is bad for both of you. Then make a concerted effort to let them go and take pride in the excellent parenting you provided.

Consider yourself as a whole

List your problems in the correct sequence so you can start addressing them and making progress. Every process requires time, and each person has unique requirements and problems. The issues described did not arise overnight, and neither will they be fixed overnight. On a t-sheet, write down your fears and concerns on one side and the things you can do to start the healing process by easing your worry and discomfort on the other. This is a useful method to pinpoint the difficulties or worries that are bothering you the most right now and are causing you the most stress, overwhelm, or depression. We are not getting any younger so now is the time to take the steps to make positive changes in our lives.

Ways to manage your debt

For some this will not apply as you have managed your debts, invested wisely and have made ample amounts of income where you have been blessed. For others, this may not be your reality. The gloom and doom of living paycheck to paycheck and feeling dead broke is no way to exist. While being in debt may seem like the end of your life; it really isn't. You don't have to live with it forever, but you have to get your priorities straight, regain control over your finances, and eliminate your debt once and for all.

Here are some steps by Irby (2021) that immensely

helped me stay on track with a solid plan and goal to get out of debt:

1. **Recognize the kind of debt you have:** To get out of something, you need to know where it's coming from to kill the root of the problem. The same is the case with your debt. Understanding why its accumulated can help you plan better and avoid repeating whatever is causing it. Your debt can be due to the loans you may have taken at a certain point in life (for a mortgage, business, school etc.), the circumstances which may have made you obtain the loan (medical, personal, or payday loans), or your habit of overspending on things you don't necessarily need.

2. **Exercise Financial Self-Control:** Regardless of how your predicament was caused, if you maintain strict control over your spending and finances, you will find it simpler to begin paying off your debt. Spend some time comparing your monthly revenue to your outgoings. Organize your spending into required/necessities (such as food, mortgage, child support) and optional/wants (such as cable TV, gym membership, entertainment) expenditures.

Your monthly costs must be much less than your monthly income to begin paying off your debt. You might be able to accomplish this by simply cutting back on your optional expenditures.

If that isn't enough, you might need to rein further in your spending by reducing your necessary expenses using tactics like renting out a room, splitting the internet with neighbors, using public transport, etc.

After you've cut your expenditure as much as you can, make a budget. This will save you from unintentionally going over budget. Ensure your costs are less than your income to avoid accruing more debt

3. **Determine your level of debt:** It can be easy to lose sight of the total amount of debt you have and the monthly interest payments you make if you have more than one sort of debt. But until you are aware of these numbers, you cannot start repaying what you owe.

Make a list of all your debts, the amount you owe at the moment, and the interest rate. To compile a comprehensive list of all the people you owe money to and their respective balances, use current billing bills, canceled checks, bank statements, and your credit report. Include the minimum payment needed for each account, as appropriate. The smallest monthly payment you can make toward your debt is this amount.

4. **Determine Your Capacity to Pay:** It may take years or even decades to pay off your debt if you merely make the minimum payment each month. You must pay more than the minimum amount due on at least one of your accounts each month if you want to pay off your debt considerably more quickly.

Determine how much you can spend each month on

debt payback using your monthly budget. Add up all your expenses, including any one-time or recurring costs that may arise during the month, and subtract them from your income. The money you have left over after paying for all necessary expenses is what you can use to pay down your debt. Use this sum in your debt-reduction strategy.

You must first deduct each minimum payment from the amount you have allocated in your budget for debt repayment since you must make the required minimum payment on each loan each month. Anything left over can be used to finish paying off your debt.

5. **Construct a Plan:** Choose the order in which you will pay off your loan. You can determine how to order your priorities depending on the interest rate, balance, or other factors. Additional debt management techniques might be used to lower monthly payments or consolidate debt.

To prevent additional fees and interest charges, follow your plan and deliver payments on time each month, regardless of your debt repayment option. Depending on your debt and how much you pay each month, it may take several months or years to pay off all of your debt. To successfully get out of debt, you must be consistent with your payments. Here are some methods you can follow:

- Pay off your debts in order of size, from smallest to largest. Pay the minimum amount owed on each bill, then apply any additional funds you may have to the debt with the lowest balance. You can notice instant results in your debt reduction by paying off this one the quickest.

- The cost of debt increases with the rate of interest. The most money can be saved over time by paying off the debt with the highest interest rate, so prioritize debt according to the interest rate. Pay the minimum amount owed on all of your debts, then apply any additional funds you may have to the debt with the highest interest rate.

- 6. **Create a fund for emergencies:** You should begin saving money for an emergency fund as you progress in paying off your debt. You'll have greater flexibility to address unforeseen costs if you build an emergency fund, which lowers your risk of future debt. It is a good feeling to have money set aside for rainy days.

The need to visit the doctor or get your car repaired can spring up at any time. This emergency fund will lessen your need to incur further credit card debt or payday loans if unplanned expenses emerge.

7. **Avoid accruing more debt:** Debt accumulation when you're trying to pay off debt may hinder your progress and generate additional interest that you will not be capable of repaying. Avoid using your credit

cards, getting new credit, or getting loans while you're trying to pay off your current debt.

If you believe you won't be able to resist using your credit cards, you might elect to close your accounts completely. However, you can also have a credit card on hand for unplanned expenses ONLY and avoid using it frequently.

8. Recover From Failure: On the way to becoming debt-free, things can not go as planned. You might have to temporarily reduce your higher payment if you have a financial emergency. It's possible that you'll need to use credit cards or obtain a personal loan to deal with an unexpected circumstance. When that occurs, reevaluate your spending plan and resume your payments as soon as you can. Avoid giving up and continue with your debt payback plan.

Setting debt repayment milestones could keep you motivated and focused during the process. You may make it simpler to stay motivated to pay off your debt by celebrating little victories like paying off your first loan or paying off 10% of your overall debt. A small reward for a job well done can be a nice way to pat yourself on the back.

Visualize placing hundreds of dollars in your trash bucket and tossing it away. Now visualize generating the income you need to pay down debt, attain security and sleep at night. Apart from these strategies, you could also consider renting out rooms in your home to increase income or turning your home into a bed and breakfast or an Air B&B. To rebuild my credit and income I rented out two to three rooms in my home on a long-term basis. Although it wasn't always simple for me as a single woman, it is one proposal for your survival as a possibility if you find yourself in a circumstance similar to mine. I decided to rent out individual rooms, making the common areas, kitchen, and bathrooms available to my tenants. To feel secure, I made a space in my house into a distinct area with locked entrances and exits. Was it ideal? Absolutely not! Was it a huge adjustment? MOST DEFINITELY! In the long run, was it beneficial to me? Yes!

Investigate background checks in depth when you are taking this route. Know your landlord/house share rights when it comes to renting out a room in your home, and get several recommendations. Although I advertised for "The Golden Girls," the people I encountered most frequently were males who had been uprooted by divorce. I chose to step out in faith and accept renters but always ask for several personal and professional recommendations. God, knows I could write another book just on the experience of renting out rooms in my home! Renters came and left for the time they needed to get back on their feet, turning my property into what I called a "healing house." I consider myself fortunate because, I didn't have many problems with my tenants over the years and this did increase revenue to achieve my end goals. I was able to pay double payments on the principal to pay down my mortgage and eliminate all debt other than running bills. I felt more secure knowing I had an affordable roof over my head.

Find value in your home in empty rooms and other buildings on your property. If you have a barn, a large garage, empty sheds or an empty lot you can rent out parking space or storage space that my be an option. Maybe you can sub-divide your property to pay down debt? Look for spaces and value in your home to utilize so you can boost your stability and income.Do you have antiques up in the attic covered in dust that can be sold or refurbished? This may very well resolve financial problems while restoring your credit and your life if you are at the empty nest stage in life and dealing with a tough financial situation. Additionally, use your own income to reduce your debt and save while collecting rent to cover your mortgage. You might want to evict some of the less desirable renters if your situation improves and you no longer require a house full of tenants.

Another option is to **keep a dependable long-term tenant** whose agreement to rent from you is advantageous for both parties. You can trade for household chores like mowing the yard, trash pickup, and repairs. Due to a positive tenant/landlord-homeowner relationship that has developed through time, the individual may also be pleasant to have around for company and someone to look over the house if you plan to travel.

I advise you **get a "tenant at will" lease** so you can evict them with a 30-day notice if things don't work out. Additionally, take a security deposit to cover any potential broken items, repair charges, and cleaning expenses. In order to ensure that the money owed to them can be given back, the security deposit should be kept in a separate account. Rules need to be adhered to regarding cleanliness, no guests in the house during the day or overnight, respect for others and timely payments are expected.

I was desperate for a solution, needing an increase in income. I listened to a sermon on television about searching your home for "hidden gems". Feeling agitated and desperate, I had a very frank conversation with God, telling him, "Lord, I have no treasures in my attic or in my basement." Then in the stillness, I heard a very loud, audible voice clamoring in my ears, "ROOMS!" That was my answer so I stepped out in faith and acted on it. At present, my house is solely in my name, I was able to rewrite for a lower interest saving me thousands of dollars over the life of the loan and decreased my monthly payments substantially. This gave me the option to apply on the principal to further decrease what I owe. I am not upside down as I managed to hold on for the market to rebound, and I actually owe very little on it. I no longer have tenants, and I maintain an excellent credit rating after battling a marital bankruptcy. Even if the trip was long, bumpy at times, and far from perfect, it was an answer to my troubles.

Trust me, I understand the very thought of sharing your living space with strangers can be uncomfortable, but I believe it is undoubtedly better than drowning in debt while coping with the changes brought on by divorce during the empty nest, and as I said, it is an option to ponder.

Here are some pros and cons you can consider to decide better for yourself (Nicely, 2020):

Pros of renting a room

- The capacity to quickly pay off your mortgage
- Additional funds to pay for home improvements and maintenance
- An additional set of hands to assist with chores
- A better sense of security if you live alone now
- Someone to look after your animals while you're away

Cons of renting a room

- If you don't know your roommate, there may be safety concerns.
- A potentially unpleasant living environment
- Concerns about theft or harm
- Unfamiliar visitors that the renter invited over.
- Opposing personalities or lifestyles

If you still have other people living in your house, make sure you discuss the decisions with anyone in your home, as renting rooms out affects others. You don't want more to deal with on your plate, so it's best to be on the same page with everyone else.

How to Rebuild your Credit

Having a strategy is a crucial first step in repairing your credit. Even though each person's situation is unique, there are some practical tactics to take into account.

Here are seven suggestions to aid credit repair (*Tips on Rebuilding Your Credit*, 2022):

- **Examine your credit report**

Many things can affect your credit score. Understanding what is on your credit report will enable you to ascertain your current situation. You may get a basic idea of your creditworthiness from your credit score. But a lot more information can be found in your credit report.

- **Dispute any errors found and update all information**

The key factor affecting your credit score is your payment history. Damaging information from your payment history, such as late or missed credit card payments, may have a long-term impact on your credit score. Other repercussions, such as late payment fines, may also result from missed payments. However, more recent information may have greater weight than previous unfavorable material. Your payment history will therefore improve the longer you pay your payments on time. And the better your credit score will be as a result.

To help you remember to pay your expenses, you can look into setting up a budget, automatic payments, or reminder alerts. Additionally, keeping your credit accounts current and in good standing requires you to make at least the minimum payment on credit accounts like your credit card. However, bear in mind that paying merely the minimum amount due could have other detrimental repercussions on your credit score.

- **Pay all bills on time to eventually remove past negative credit**

You should catch up on any payments that are past due from not paying them on time. You may take various actions to catch up on your credit card payments if you've fallen behind.

If you're having trouble paying your debts, you can also think about getting in touch with your creditors. They could possibly assist you with a payment plan.

- **Achieve authorized user status**

If you know someone with a good credit score who trusts you and you can trust, they can add you as an authorized user to their account. Although payment obligations ultimately rest with the primary account holder, you can still buy things now, thanks to this. Additionally, their proper use can raise your credit score and help you develop credit, that too, without fulfilling any requirements to apply or run a credit check in order to be an authorized user.

- **Get a secured credit card**

A secured credit card could be beneficial as you rebuild your credit. It works the same way as a regular credit card in that you can make purchases. But because you have to pay a security deposit to open the account, it is regarded as being "secured."

Some credit card providers notify the credit bureaus about your status when you have a secured card. Therefore, if you're using your card properly and making at least your minimum payment on time, it could help you rebuild credit. A car loan is secured and may also be a way to re-establish credit if you are driving a vehicle that is getting tired and you need a car that is newer with less mileage and years.

- **Use less than 30% of the credit**

Credit utilization is another term for how much of your available credit you are using. This is crucial since maintaining a credit usage rate below 30% might demonstrate that you are using credit wisely and refraining from excessive expenditure.

- **Keep track of your advancement**

Consider using a credit monitoring tool like CreditWise from Capital One as you attempt to raise your credit score. Everyone can utilize this free tool. You'll receive alerts when there are significant changes to your TransUnion credit report.

Apply some of these reliable tactics to start working on becoming an overcomer. Choose what works best for you. It may be hard to start reorganizing your life, finances, and relationships all over again but much of your concerns will eventually be resolved and removed from your list, helping you emerge from this chapter of life healthier and happier with an improved sense of security. Maintain a laser-beam focus and diligent effort, and watch while good things come (read: run) to you.

CHAPTER 4: WHAT NOW?

Your interests and life were placed on hold for more than 18- 20 years while you adopted the role of a selfless giver. But in this chapter of your new life, it is time to think about yourself, and while you are at it, jot it all down in your to-do list. Ask yourself, who was I before having children? What hobbies or interests did I have? How did I spend my time? What healthful activities can you engage in to make the most of your newly found freedom?

You could join support groups, form your own meet-up or Facebook group, join an existing group, volunteer, reconnect with old friends, find new friends who share your interests, join a gym, participate in church activities, and perhaps join a travel group; the possibilities are limitless.

Just remember, you are where you are because of the decisions you made or didn't make. Most of these decisions didn't involve what you wanted, they revolved around what would be better for your family as a whole. Now, you have all the freedom to think about what adjustments you must make if you want a happy, meaningful life. Don't let this precious phase go to waste. This is the time for YOU to think about YOU!

Let's jump right into exploring your options – the things you can add to your to-do list!

Here are some ideas you can consider, outlined by Ashraf (2019) and Jane (n.d.):

Remodel your home's decor

Your home is a representation of all the members that live in it, it encapsulates each individual's personality, and so, yours may have been a mix of you and your kids. Now that your house is empty, redo it your way. As you look around, you see cracks in the horsehair sheet rock, a well-worn house in need of paint, a couch with pills and tears, stained carpeting, tile missing the grout, outdated wallpaper and the like. It is time for repairs and a facelift.It goes without mention you may have to start small but even fresh new paint can make an enormous difference and brighten things up. Add colors and things that help you feel relaxed and calm, or experiment with furniture that you may have never been able to have before. If it is clear the kids are not coming back home you may want to mention plans to redo their rooms. Allow them to store away or take anything they may want from the house before you begin with the makeover.

Here are 10 home improvement tips you could utilize if you're wishing to redecorate your home (Nicole, n.d.):

1. **Establish a Budget**: set a budget, include a contingency, and then include that contingency once more. Whether you are spending thousands of dollars or only a few hundred dollars, do this. This will help you when making decisions on finishes and materials as the project progresses, assisting you in maintaining project control.

2. **Future-proofing:** because of the clutter, the cost, and the laborious nature of major house modifications when a family is living there— they don't happen very often. Can you remember the last time you introduced upgrades to your house while considering your future needs? If the answer is "never" or "it's been quite a while," this is the time to modify your housekeeping with at least your next 20 years in mind.

3. **Resolve any pending issues:** Before starting any cosmetic repair on your property, you should address any potential structural issues, such as dampness, heating issues, roof difficulties, rotten wood etc. Building issues

never go away on their own, therefore it pays to hire an expert surveyor to provide you with advice on how to deal with them for good. Additionally, fixing one problem might unleash another. For example my plan to sand and repaint my porch uncovered rotten supports and some wooden planks and rails that needed to be replaced. So, consider your budget accordingly.

4. **Reconsider how you plan to use your area**: there are countless ways to reconfigure a house's original footprint. You have the option to extend, knock through, or convert. If it's a large job, you'll need expert guidance from an architect who can provide many suggestions as well as ensure that it complies with building codes and other tedious requirements. Generally, spare rooms with neutral design are more practical and can accommodate all of your visitors, including your children's partners, your future grandkids, and even your workspace needs. My children's rooms are now beautiful guest rooms for them when they decide to come visit.

5. **One-time investment:** invest all you can in buying the basics for your home, like tiles, furniture, and fittings. The better quality you buy, the longer it will last you. In fact, you may never even have to replace it again. Keep

in mind, you are not the youngster you used to be, so it's likely you won't have the motivation to re-do your home later anyways. Solid hardwoods, leather, porcelain, stone, marble, and high-quality fixtures and fittings are some examples of materials that will pay for themselves over time.

6. **Remember to ventilate and insulate:** a well-insulated home uses less energy and is more pleasant to live in. Heat rises, so make sure your loft insulation is deep enough. It's simple to install and very affordable, but it may significantly lower heat loss and heating costs. However, homes that have been well-insulated can get stuffy, locking in humidity and lowering air quality. So, it's crucial to have a steady flow of fresh air moving around. You can install humidity fans in the kitchen and bathroom to prevent condensation, and passive air vents to promote airflow to keep mold issues at bay.

7. **Choose your style:** by the time we reach midlife, the majority of us have amassed a sizable amount of stuff that, to be honest, we don't particularly adore; it had a purpose, but it was never really a part of a design strategy. It's time to conduct a small inventory and select what you love, what you want to maintain, and what you vehemently despise. Offer unneeded items for sale or give them to

one of the many charities that will distribute them to deserving households. Discovering what your ideal home would seem like can amaze you with how much fun it is.

8. **Remodel and reuse:** in today's world, it is important to make sustainable choices to reduce harm to the environment. Reupholstering a beloved sofa rather than throwing it away not only supports regional artisan enterprises but also preserves traditional skills. Look around your house or search for old furniture online, you might be able to find numerous pieces you could remodel in your own way to include in your home.

9. **Include elements of sensory input:** The goal of home modification is to set the stage for the life we envision and dream about. Add elements that appeal to your senses, like the crackling fire from the fire pit. Consider every detail of your home; doing so will make it unique to you. By the time we reach middle age, we should all be aware of what brings us joy. Just remember not to replicate someone else's dream; while it may appear fantastic in a high-end publication, it is not worth it if it doesn't please you.

10. **Bring the greens inside:** you can hang plant pots or grow a vertical garden that climbs up your wall to add a pop of nature inside your

house. It can revitalize your senses and refresh your mood just by looking at it. You could also add greenery to your balcony or install big windows in your revamped house to get a better view of the garden outside, without actually having to bring any plants indoors.

Adopt a pet

If you are not willing to give up your motherly responsibilities just yet, adopting a pet is a great way to keep them since pets are no less than having children. An added bonus is having company while also keeping busy with their upkeep.

Learn a foreign language

For some, learning a new language is a fantastic way to expand one's horizons and mentally challenge yourself. For me, not so much! You can purchase audible books where you can learn words and phrases while driving. You'll be able to communicate with more people, read more literature, watch more TV and movies, learn vocabulary that the English language simply does not have, and use your time in a really productive way.

Experience different cuisines

If you are a foodie, get out of your comfort zone and try new cuisines. Rather than cooking you could visit a restaurant nearby with a menu completely unfamiliar to you, or you can make traveling a fantastic time to sample out diverse cuisines from around the world. If you are the daring type, exploring some astonishingly cheap and delectable food on the streets of practically any major city is a brilliant way to try out the local cuisine there. For example, I live near Boston so taking a trip to China Town or the North End for authentic Italian cuisine could make for a fun weekend away. NYC is loaded with awesome restaurants to with lots of diversity with authentic cooking.

Volunteering

Reaching out and providing assistance to those in need is an amazing approach to overcoming heartache. The happiness you get by being of use to someone who needs you is incomparable to anything else. It makes you feel happier, more confident, and more purposeful (Hughes, 2011). Look around you. Do you know an older person who needs company or some groceries? A neighbor experiencing difficulty? A teacher who requires an additional set of hands in the classroom? You can find many volunteering opportunities if you begin to look for them. During sad times in my life, when I was in my classroom teaching and giving to others, I forgot my problems. My troubles virtually disappeared and only returned driving to and from work. Keeping busy is medicine to the soul when taking your eyes off yourself and you focus on others.

Travel

The ideal time to start making travel arrangements to destinations you have always wanted to see is when you have an empty nest. No kids to worry about, no added responsibilities, and the complete liberty to do as you want. Increasing income can transform your wishful, someday bucket lists into becoming realities and dreams coming true.

Also, the excitement that comes with anticipating a vacation and arranging for it is almost as enjoyable as taking it! So the fun begins even before your travel does.

According to a survey conducted by Peregrine (n.d.), over 20% of respondents named "spending time in a tropical beach resort" as their top travel want, while 19% are eager to cross items off their travel wish list and another 19% yearn for a romantic break with their significant other.

Keeping the above-given statistics in mind, here are some places you can visit inexpensively with Intrepid Travel (a travel company with great packages) (Peregrine, n.d.):

1. **Romantic getaway to Southern Spain and Morocco:** This two-week trip is the ideal getaway for couples because it offers beautiful scenery, well-preserved fortifications, vibrant medinas, delicious food, and much more. Explore the colorful squares of Granada, take in the atmosphere of Seville as the city comes to life at night, hike through historic woodlands and steep terrain in Grazalema National Park (formerly visited by Romans, Moors, and bandits), and

then fly to Morocco for a real feast for the senses.

2. **Kenya Lodge Safari:** Discover the lush plains of the wildlife-rich Aberdare National Park and Lake Nakuru, converse with a Maasai tribe about daily life in the Masai Mara, and take in the stunning sunsets over the savanna from the comfort of your luxury tented campsite. This is the perfect opportunity to live out your childhood fantasy of being in The Lion King.

3. **Explore the culture of Italy and Southern France:** When kids are in the mood for a vacation, there's a high chance they won't be big fans of visiting the museums for as long as you would have wanted to. However, you don't have to worry about that anymore. This trip can be an ideal introduction to Europe for empty nesters, who will be joined by a group of like-minded travelers, led by a knowledgeable local guide who'll show you the must-see locations (as well as some hidden treasures).

4. **Beach escapes to Belize and Guatemala:** One of the most picturesque places on earth is on Mexico's east coast, which features sun-drenched beaches, snow-white sands, and breathtaking seaside ruins. Explore the ruins of ancient Maya cities in the Guatemalan highlands with a knowledgeable local guide,

spend the night in an eco-lodge in the jungle, stroll through the vibrant streets of World Heritage-listed cities, and learn about the vibrancy and beauty of Central America to make the most of your trip.

5. **Cruising in Antarctica:** It's unlike anything else on Earth to have the opportunity to travel alongside enormous glaciers, be caught in penguin rush hour on a freezing beach, or see colonies of seals basking on rocky outcrops. Travel in style on Peregrine Adventures' strong super-yacht, the Ocean Diamond, which has roomy cabins with private en suites and views of the outside. Their knowledgeable captains, officers, expedition leaders, and guides will be by your side every nautical mile of the journey.

If you're looking to travel independently, without being accompanied by a group, here are some additional destinations by Ashraf (2018) you can consider Madeira: Madeira is an archipelago ruled by Portugal that is about 320 miles off the coast of Africa and about an hour and a half by plane from Lisbon. It's a well-liked holiday spot all year round due to its temperate climate, which combines an isolated location, subtropical island weather, and beaches with European cuisine and culture. Numerous hotels reside all over the island, some of which include an oceanfront setting, lovely gardens, a spa, and a rooftop pool.

1. **Montenegro:** Located on the Adriatic Sea, Montenegro is a tiny nation distinguished by magnificent beaches, breathtaking mountain vistas, and charming ancient towns. As the Balkan country heals and revives following the Yugoslavian civil war of the 1990s, tourists are rediscovering it. You'll find glacial lakes, limestone peaks, a 4,265-foot-deep canyon, and the Bay of Kotor – one of the world's most attractive locations famed for its breathtaking views.

2. **Panama City:** The capital of Panama, known as "the Dubai of Latin America," is a booming metropolis with skyscrapers, a burgeoning rich population, and a vibrant restaurant and entertainment scene. Pay a visit to the Panama Canal where you can ride a boat or just watch them pass by or consider taking a luxurious train down the canal or going to the Miraflores Visitors Center, which has an excellent museum if you'd prefer to view the iconic landmark from a more dry location.

3. **Turkish Riviera:** The Turkish Riviera, also known as the Turquoise Coast due to its breathtakingly blue waters, is a coastal region in southwest Turkey with more than 600 miles of breathtaking coastline along the Aegean and Mediterranean Seas. It is home to world-class beaches, mountain scenery, and a pleasant climate. Two of the Seven Wonders

of the Ancient World's ruins, the Mausoleum of Mausollos and the Temple of Artemis, are located in this area, giving the area a strong historical presence. However, modern civilization is also leaving its mark, as new hotels are springing up for travelers looking for a place to stay.

Adventuring with your partner

If you are seeking some adventurous trips to embark on with your other half, you can seek inspiration from Veronica and David, a couple who sold everything purchased an RV, and explored the entire United States. After their last child graduated, they sold everything they owned and bought an RV from eBay to drive across the country in order to catch up with missed visits that they had been putting off for so long. They enjoyed it so much that after they were done meeting everyone, they chose to continue traveling. They have since been to all 50 states and 53 different countries, started a popular travel blog, and written a best-selling book about their experiences (Empty Nest, 2019). If they can do it, why can't you? As they say, "You Are Never Too Old To Set Another Goal Or To Dream A New Dream" C. S Lewis.

Day trips

During my empty nest phase, I went on day trips with my friends since I was on a strict budget. If you're from New Hampshire, you can check out my book on Amazon, "Eat Drink See NH: A Pocket Travel Guide for Day Trips in NH" to seek inspiration and help planning your trips. For those of you from another state, you could look for local events in the paper or the "places recommended" section on your state's website. You may also want to start a Meet-up or a Facebook page so people can share places they enjoyed in your state. This is a great way to learn things about your state you didn't already know. Road trips on weekends, planned within your budget is a great way to feel satisfied bringing new adventures and experiences to your life.

Cooking

You may be used to feeding your family every night, considering your children's tastes and their likes and dislikes while preparing meals and shopping for groceries. It took me a very long time to cut down on my grocery list as I still had the mindset of cooking for a family. I would inevitably overcook and freeze the left overs in 1 -2 portion meals sizes for days I did not want to cook for myself. With the house to yourself, you can now cook to satisfy you (and your spouse's) tastebuds. Expand your horizons and share your collection of crockpot recipes, Cooking on a Dime, and 100 meals with chicken or ground beef with your kids now that they are try out their cooking skills on lean budgets. Try out new recipes, spice up your life and experiment in your kitchen, you never know when you might create a masterpiece. Even if the picture looks better than it tastes, you won't have to listen to the grumbling of kids, and you will have tried something different.

Gardening

A garden is a wonderful area to concentrate your efforts and feel successful. When you plant a seed, nurture it with love and see it transition into a full-grown plant brimming with life, the feeling of fulfillment is out of this world. It's much like seeing your children succeed in life as a result of your hard work. And of course, the soothing and calming effects of breathing in nature can never be underestimated. I knew I was finding my way to recovery and loving my home once again once my gardens began blooming with life and color. During the beginning stages of the empty nest phase, I had no desire to pull weeds, plant or prune. My gardens looked sad as I let the weeds in, and its state was a reflection of how I felt inside-miserable! Once I began repairing patios, adding a fire pit and planting again, my house became a welcoming refuge, full of color, life and comfort. The curb appeal returned, and my deserted gardens became my happy place once again. My flourishing gardens brought back color, life, hummingbirds, bees and butterflies. I began falling in love with my passion for gardening and my efforts brought me a newfound appreciation for the simple things in life.

Scrapbooking/Memory Book

is a creative and entertaining project you can undertake to preserve priceless memories, collect mementos, and release your creative side. Throughout your life, you may have taken pictures of your favorite things, collected cards or drawings your children made, and captured some of your favorite places that you visited. It's time to put them all into a scrapbook. Even if you don't have any available material, you can begin collecting some. This will be a delight to look at later on in life. I pulled apart photographs that were discoloring from age and scanned my favorites on my computer. You may want to create memory books with companies such as Shutterfly or Google Pics among others. It is a great way to keep memories and events organized and save photographs from the destruction of acidic photo book pages turning your photographs brown, and ruining your pictures. I uploaded favorite photographs of each of my children and grandchildren, and created books for myself. I also created books of my friends, my accomplishments, places I have visited and events that are special to me. Sending zip lock bags of assorted photographs for each of your children to sort and keep is a way to declutter and share the memories with your children. Rather than having pictures of your children in every room, I made a grandma and me frame with string and used mini clothespins to hang pics of my grandchildren and I. I also updated pictures of each of my children with their families, and stored older pictures, baby books, teeth, little curls found in first hair cut envelopes and favorite school creations in a large trunk filled with dated zip-locked baggies filled to the brim with pictures that tell stories over the years all safely packed, and in one area. I think of it as organizing the chapters of my life with new exciting adventures to add to my fondest memory collections.

Read Positive affirmations daily

Positive affirmations are words or phrases that are used to refute unfavorable or negative ideas. They are the ideal way to use your thinking, which is your most effective instrument, to remind yourself of all the good things in your life. Daily, I would profess, "I am the King's daughter, I am blessed and highly favored." I would and still profess the same over my children's lives and believe it. These encouraging affirmations, and prophetic words spoken out loud will set the tone for your day. With time and experience, you'll discover that they're not only comforting but also an important part of your day, and your way of life. Make it a habit to be grateful and think good thoughts.

Get a motorcycle license and cruise around

Breaking out of your comfort zone can be tough, but once you defeat whatever is holding you back, you feel a sense of confidence that is incomparable to anything else. Cruising around on your motorcycle after getting your license can bring a new wave of adventure into your life. It's a great way to pass your time and the thrill cannot be described in words as you shift and maneuver down the road. I have girlfriends who are seasoned riders however it takes time to be a confident skilled rider. I did get my license and decided I would rather be a passenger than the driver. After taking short trips on country roads to practice my skills with hands clenched, knuckles white, eyes searching for loose gravel, darting kids, dogs, deer, and drivers who pull out in front of you, I found it added too much stress so it was not for me. However, I pat myself on the back for trying something new and surviving my attempt to try something new.

Do a make-over/ facial/massage

Your self-confidence and esteem may have hit an all-time low undergoing this empty nest phase in your life. Getting a makeover and taking care of yourself can make you feel more confident by putting your concerns aside. You may also feel more in control when you know you can always choose something for yourself, no matter how trivial makeup or a facial may seem in the grand scheme of things. Everyone likes to feel like they look at their best. As alien as it may feel to pamper yourself- do it! Getting a new hairstyle, a new hair color, a facial, new make-up and wardrobe can be a huge "pick me" up, and something long overdue. I remember wearing everybody's hand me downs including my ex- mother-in-laws polyester pull on pants and sweatshirts! I was way overdue for a complete make-over, dressing stylishly and spending money on myself. All kidding aside, no wonder I wound up divorced!!

Start a weekly board game night with neighbors

Building strong social ties helps us become more resilient, improves our physical and mental health, and enables us to handle stress in daily life (Ottowa Public Health, n.d.). And what's a better way of doing so than by indulging in weekly board games? Some people enjoy weekly card games too! Even BINGO beats sitting home alone and who knows, you may win!

Be grateful

The best method to improve your attitude is to feel thankful for what you have. Take the time to think about how amazing it is that you were able to create wonderful, independent individuals, and be thankful for that. You cared for them and chauffeured them in many carpools; now they are off to study, chasing the road to success. Also, aren't you grateful for less laundry and chores?! I definitely am. Scribble down your accomplishments and read how far you have come. Everyday is a new victory no matter how small the steps are that you have taken thus far. Bottom line, celebrate even little victories as you have come a long way, baby!!

Learn something new

Learning a new skill, such as knitting, pottery, stained glass, drawing, etc., can make you feel more useful and fill up your day with something to do. Plus, it's always great to have a bunch of skills at your disposal and meet others with similar interests. After all, you never know when you may be needing them. This could lead into a new side job or even creating personal homemade gifts for holidays.

More on the kind of skills great for empty nester's, you can learn in the next chapter.

Exercise ideas for women aged 40-50:

As you grow older, you may have noticed a decline in your motivation to exercise and work on yourself.

However, physical activity is extremely essential to keep the body healthy, while inactivity can put you at risk of chronic diseases (Mayer, 2022).

Here are a few exercises you can try to prevent the following health issues (Rabbitt, 2017):

- Hold a plank for 90 seconds, three times a week, to relieve back pain.
- Do yoga once a week as a way to combat depression.
- Strength training two to three times a week to combat arthritis.
- Engage in high-impact activities, one to two times a week to prevent osteoporosis.
- Practice cardiovascular exercises three to four times per week to prevent heart disease.

I do not like to exercise, I actually hate it. I think I would rather go to the dentist than the gym however walking works for me. During the winter I do not care for the cold, dangers of ice or dogs so I prefer to walk in malls or on a treadmill. During the summer, I like to walk on school track fields because they are gated and use a rubberized material so it is easier on my feet. This is a great way to lose weight and tone up without killing yourself. If you find a friend to walk with you all the better. If you get up at 5am and walk until 7am, get home, take a shower and head out for work you will feel great starting your day. I actually gained a nice tan effortlessly by walking in the early summer mornings.

Learn about yourself

Lastly and most importantly, take this time to learn about yourself. Your interests may have changed over the course of years, but due to a lack of time, you may have not realized that. This test (www.almostemptynest/empty-nest-super-power-quiz) is a great way to figure out your likes and dislikes.

N ow that you (have more than) a bunch of things for you to start jotting down on your to-do list, what are you waiting for? Get started!

CHAPTER 5: ME, MYSELF & I

You already have a list of things to do to distract your mind and fill your day up. But that's not all, it's time for you to bring a change to the career aspect of your life as well.

As the main caregiver, you experience a sense of worthlessness and needlessness in addition to being lost and confused. Aside from losing interests and pastimes, you also need to determine your identity and purpose. Yes, you were so and so's mom for the longest time, but it's time to focus on your work now. As Kim Alexis says, "The biggest change for me as a mom was realizing I needed to put someone else before me. Now the hardest part about the empty nest is learning to put me first." But if not now, then when?

You could potentially begin a new career, return to school, or, if you are retired, perhaps you could volunteer. Ask yourself, "Is my job satisfying?" "Do I want to spend the rest of my life doing this?" "Am I feeling safe?" "Do I want to pursue a different line of work?" "Need I get a job?" "Do I require training in job skills?"

Speaking with as many people as you can about their occupations and deciding what you like is one of the finest ways to make this determination. Parenting has given many women a ton of new hobbies and talents. Achievements and skill-builders that can lead to a new job include managing a travel soccer team, organizing fundraisers for your child's school, and working on home improvement projects (Emptynest, 2021).

Moreover, your financial situation may be tough on you right now. And of course, the first thing that can change it around is a consistent salary earned through working a job. Assess your situation thoroughly! Some empty nesters are in better situations than others, so the degree of work will vary depending on each individual's circumstances.

However, at this point in your life, don't just work for the sake of it. Most of us have done that all our lives in order to fulfill the financial responsibilities we have toward our families. Now is the time for you to work for yourself, satisfy your needs, and bring yourself some inner satisfaction.

Let's begin exploring your options!

Career advice for empty nesters

The best course of action, if you're considering returning to the workforce, is to reevaluate your objectives and motivation, create a strategy, and polish your skills. The time is now to take it easy, take care of yourself, and accept new challenges. Here are some tips to help you make the right decision (Voll, 2022):

1. **Don't rush:** Returning to the employment may be a difficult lifestyle change for empty-nester mothers, especially after a long sabbatical. Try to accept this new normal and exercise patience as you look for a new routine that suits you.

The days of constantly having to be on the move are over. Spend some time slowing down and carefully consider your objectives. Take out that journal that has been gathering dust, and start writing down some of your feelings and thoughts. You'll be able to hear your inner wishes more clearly if you take the time to unwind and become aware of your breath.

2. **Analyze the circumstances:** Take a career or personality evaluation to discover your hidden talents and qualities that could lead you to your ideal job. What do you want to accomplish as you continue this new chapter? It's probable that the objectives you set 18 years ago have altered, and that's normal. Now is the moment to think about and become inquisitive about the things you've wanted to pursue but haven't had the time to prioritize. Do you want to volunteer for a certain cause or attend a class that you have been longing to take? You'll be able to better grasp what path you might want to take in your profession if you spend some time exploring.

3. **List everything down:** Make a list of all the talents you have acquired, both at work and outside of it, as well as your weaknesses, and strengths. You've been the CFO of your house for a while, and the talents you've developed there are transferable to a variety of jobs. When you put pen to paper, jot down everything that comes to mind. This will assist you as you plan how to proceed with coaching, update your abilities, and create a résumé.

Don't be afraid to challenge yourself because you may be a great fit for numerous occupations with your wealth of experience, emotional stability, and specific expertise. Consider carefully what you want to do with this time in your life. Then, update your LinkedIn profile and search for jobs in the industries you're interested in. Pay close attention to your transferable skills, which can be applied to practically any field and should be listed on your resume and cover letter. Examples of these skills include communication and management. This will demonstrate to the hiring manager that you have the skills necessary for the job

4. **Figure out what's keeping you from achieving your full potential.**

Do you often contemplate, "I haven't had a job in so long, who would want to hire me?" Working with a coach or mentor can help you change the untrue stories you tell yourself in this situation. In order for you to start seeing all that you can give a company, a coach can question your views. You will acquire tools that will enable you to improve your self-worth and confidence as you progress through the coaching process.

5. **Abandon comparisons with others.**

We are each on our own trip, moving at our own rates of pace and toward distinct destinations. Life is vibrant because of this. Each of us has certain talents and life experiences to share. Your journey will be a flowing river with many currents rather than a straight line from one place to another (how dull would that be?). It's time for us to relax on our float and accept the shifting currents and directions. The more you unwind and relish the experience, the more likely it is that you will recognize and discover a profession that is genuinely your dream job.

6. **Boost your skills with career-based courses.**

If you've taken a break from the workforce and are returning, you may need to retrain and return to school to bring your abilities up to speed. If you don't feel ready to accept your new route, enroll in a course online or at one of the numerous nearby schools or universities, acquire certificates, pursue a new degree, or speak with a career counselor who can assist you in creating a successful progression plan. Learning is a lifelong process that is age-neutral. Online courses are a great option, too.

7. **Engage in extensive networking.**

A job may result from relationships you create through networking. There are many possibilities available to you if you want to return to the workforce. You can get in touch with previous coworkers, make a temporary hire, or join a group for professionals in your industry. Listen to see if anyone is looking to hire or ask if anyone knows of an opportunity. Don't overlook the potential of your immediate group, which includes friends, neighbors, and the parents of your children's classmates. Most often, someone closest to us will say something that alters our perception of who we are and opens the door to a new potential. You may even enlist a friend to interview you and give you feedback afterward.

8. Discover fresh possibilities

These days, careers in technology, healthcare, finance, real estate, and administration are among the greatest jobs for empty nesters. Women Returners, a purpose-driven consulting, coaching, and network organization, can assist in locating new opportunities by providing support through special programs, events, and webinars. You might also start looking for part-time or seasonal employment, volunteer your time and efforts for a non-profit organization, or even check into positions abroad. You may be able to find a job that coincides with a degree, such as at a school, where you could work with children or maybe a nursing program where you can work as an aide. However, if you are still confused about the career to choose, you can always take a career test to unravel further possibilities for yourself.

Remember, "Your child's life will be filled with

fresh experiences. It's good if yours is as well."—Dr. Margaret Rutherford

9.Work on a new resume to account for long gaps.
Does the long, dreaded gap on your resume keep you from working again? If so, put that worry aside. This gap can be filled by volunteer work, any courses attended during that period, and more (Weinberg, 2021). Even though volunteering is not paid labor, the skills and accomplishments that come with it are just as valuable as those obtained from a job.

Even though the majority of resumes are chronological, there is a different format that is ideal for those who have a longer gap between jobs. This format is known as the functional resume (Weinberg, 2021). A functional resume structure places more emphasis on skills rather than previous work history. So, your name and contact information are followed immediately by a description of your key aptitudes and skills. This usually takes place within the framework of themes. If useful, you can utilize the job description's keywords to guide your skill categories. Then, highlight your most noteworthy experiences and accomplishments in four to five bullet points under each talent group. Instead of just describing the duties or responsibilities you've had, emphasize your effect and the outcomes you've achieved with numbers. This will leave a better impact on the employer. Your children can probably assist you in writing an updated resume and cover letter.

Top 10 Jobs for Empty Nesters

If you're a woman seeking low-stress jobs with flexible hours and the option to work from home, here are the top 10 jobs you can consider (Doyle, 2022):

Manager of Administrative Services

Managers of administrative services plan and direct the company's auxiliary services. They might manage databases, oversee administrative staff, define objectives for the administrative division, and more. Administrative Assistant, General Office Clerk, Human Resources Manager, Paralegal, Postsecondary Education Administrator, Program Coordinator, and Travel Agent are among the positions that could be filled.

Bus Driver

Bus driving services require moving pupils to school or operating a city or town's public transportation system. It's a great career for people who don't want to go back to school because most bus drivers only need a commercial driver's license and a spotless driving record. A few bus-driving businesses provide paid training. Additionally, it has flexible hours, so it's a wonderful job for someone with a hectic schedule.

As Albert Einstein says, "Life is like riding a bicycle (read: bus). To keep your balance you must keep moving".

We're taking this one a little too literally, eh? But it does make sense!

High School Teacher

If you generally love being around kids, teaching is a great profession to consider. Teachers in high school typically focus on one subject. For those who have professional experience in an area and wish to instruct students in that field, this position may be ideal. You also have flexibility with summer and other school breaks.

A bachelor's degree and a state-issued certification are typically requirements for instructors in public schools. Once they acquire a position, several states may demand that instructors obtain a master's degree. You might not need certification for jobs as a substitute teacher or in private schools.

Innkeeper

This position may be ideal for you if you like interacting with people are interested in working for yourself, and enjoy working in a team environment. Innkeepers that are successful often have a background in hospitality, business management, or both. The following positions are connected to inn keeping:

1. Event/Convention Planner
2. Farmer
3. Manager of Food Services
4. Personal Chef
5. Manager of Real Estate or Community Association
6. Tour Guide

Technician for Medical Information

Medical information technicians—also referred to as medical records and health information technicians —are responsible for organizing and managing a variety of health information data stored both electronically and in paper files. They are employed by hospitals, medical practices, nursing homes, and other places.

A certificate program or an associate degree in health information technology is often required for medical information technicians. These courses can be completed in as little as a year.

Occupational Therapist

Treatment for individuals who are hurt, ill, or disabled is provided by an occupational therapist (OT). The OT assists patients in utilizing daily tasks and in enhancing and maintaining the skills required for daily life.

More and more people need occupational therapy as the population ages. Many clients over 50 value working with OTs who are close to their own age. OTs must hold a master's degree at the very least, however many pursue a doctorate, which takes around three and a half years to complete.

Personal Financial Consultant

A personal financial consultant counsels clients on a variety of financial issues, including taxes, investments, insurance, and retirement. In order to help customers achieve their goals, the advisor provides financial management advice.

Since many financial advisors work for themselves, they can choose their own hours. Personal financial advisors are often exempt from specialized education requirements and only need a bachelor's degree.

A Real Estate Broker

Realtors assist clients in the purchase, sale, and rental of real estate. They present purchase offers, exhibit these properties to potential purchasers or tenants, and assist in mediating negotiations between the buyer (or renter) and seller. Additionally, they prepare all relevant documents and contracts.

The typical educational requirements for this position are passing a licensing exam and taking certain real estate courses. People have interpersonal and business acumen, which are both talents that can be learned in the workplace and in life, and are most suited for the position.

Licensed Nurse

Patients are cared for by registered nurses (RNs). This care may involve identifying and documenting symptoms, giving medication, working with doctors, keeping an eye on hospital equipment, and walking patients through procedures. Hospitals, doctor's offices, and nursing homes are the traditional workplaces for nurses.

People who appreciate working with and helping others will really enjoy this field. It necessitates attending school: A diploma from a nursing program, a bachelor's or associate's degree in nursing, or both are required of RNs.

Technical Writer

A technical writer contributes to the creation of written materials that convey complex technological information by writing, editing, and other preparations. How-to manuals, instruction books, journal articles, web articles, and other writings could all be produced by a technical writer.

Many technical writers are employed by particular businesses, while some also operate as freelancers for particular clients. Many female employees over 50 who want to keep a flexible schedule and perhaps work from home will find this to be ideal.

Both those with experience in writing and editing as well as those with an understanding of a particular technical discipline, such as computer science or medicine, are excellent candidates for jobs in technical writing. For those in either industry, this job makes a fantastic second career.

Fostering Children

Apart from all the conventional jobs, has your love for children ever made you consider fostering one? Of course, this is an area that requires the right reasons, passions, and skills before getting involved. These include (Craft, 2020):

Truthful Self-Evaluation

Most couples contemplate entering the foster care system for two or three years before taking the plunge. Here are some things to think about before deciding whether or not to take up foster care.

Who can become a foster parent is subject to some limitations, and each state has its own set of rules that must be followed. Check the local regulations to see if your family and home meet the standards before applying.

Moreover, successful foster parents must possess a variety of abilities, including the capacity for patience and the capacity to say goodbye.

Fostering can and probably will have an effect on your marriage, so you must be prepared for that beforehand. In fact, it will have an impact on your kids, those still left at home and even those grown, and out of the house. Being thoughtful in your planning and contemplating over the kids you plan to foster will help in preparation for future unintended consequences that may affect your family.

Communicating Effectively

As a foster parent, you will interact with a wide range of individuals, so you must be able to listen, express your viewpoint, and speak out for your foster child as well as for the rest of your family. You'll probably need to feel at ease speaking with the following people:

- Doctors
- Judges and other members of the court (like a GAL or a CASA worker)
- Most crucially, the youngster you will be fostering
- Other foster parents
- Social workers and other agency personnel
- Educators and other school personnel
- The birth parents

- Therapists
- Your loved ones and friends, who could not comprehend your foster parent's job

Possibility of Accepting Challenges

Extreme cruelty and neglect have frequently been inflicted on children in foster care. A child who has experienced trauma could engage in challenging behaviors as a means of expression and coping. Add to that the fact that the foster care system may be foreign, making it difficult for both foster parents and children to maneuver.

Think about how your first day of hosting your foster child will go and how you will transition into your new role as a foster parent. Surely it will take some time for your foster kid to settle in and feel secure in your home. Imagine how you would feel being placed in the care of total strangers?

Resolving conflicts and using constructive discipline

A well-stocked toolset of positive discipline techniques is what foster parents need to be well equipped. Observe that children are making an effort. Your foster child will need your love, support, and supervision because they might push your boundaries and disobey your rules. Parenting success is largely dependent on being ready to handle disagreement. The years of acquiring parenting skills and dealing with teens may come in handy should you decide to take on this feat.

. . .

Compassion

A child's sorrow and sadness (grieving the loss of their home and family as well as the prior abuse) can frequently lead to problematic conduct. Being compassionate to yourself and your foster child is a lifelong practice. Recognize that a child's distress or unfavorable behaviors could make them feel unfavorable about you. The youngster may have many painful feelings that they can finally express now that they are in the secure surroundings of your home. So, understand that any difficult behavior is probably not about you, and have sympathy for the difficulties your foster child has experienced. I have friends who have been foster parents, and some of the stories that they share tend to be rather colorful. The children are placed in emergency care homes being exposed to situations no child should experience, and have developed a hardened, self- survival persona. Some sadly hoard food and squirrel it away as they were victims of being hungry.

Collaboration.

You will collaborate with a wide range of experts as a foster parent to support your foster kid. Effective communication is essential for this collaboration. You might be required to participate in group meetings as a foster parent. If so, it's crucial to be ready to take part and share knowledge about the requirements of the child. Additionally, many first-time foster parents are anxious to meet the child's biological family, but you might discover that you are eventually mentoring or fostering the entire family. This is significant because the process of family reunification frequently involves foster parents in a significant way.

On the other hand, you can also discover that you are unaware of the developments in the case of your foster child. In these circumstances, it's crucial to get in touch with your kid's caseworker to learn all you can, offer your knowledge, and speak out for the needs of your foster child.

Lastly, make sure that:

- if you're married, your spouse is on board.
- you have an emotionally healthy home.
- you have a room available for each foster child as the home would have to pass safety inspections as well as background checks for all adults.
- you have looked into your state's criteria, online classes, and procedures to become a licensed foster parent.

If you live in NH, you can (Foster, 2019):
Register with FACES

Training in Foster and Adoptive Care Essentials (FACES) helps one become a capable caregiver and a capable team member. Regular training sessions are provided throughout the year for no cost. The foster care system and working with kids and their families are made clearer in FACES seminars. The lessons are primarily taught by foster and adoptive parents. You can get many of your questions answered during the first two weeks of orientation and licensing. You don't have to finish the sessions if you decide foster care isn't for you—they're a terrific place to start!

Obtain a license through an agency

Foster care licensing is offered by several organizations. They will lead you through the home study and a few inspections that are necessary for licensing. The Division for Children, Youth, and Families (DCYF) grants licenses at the state level. You need to complete an inquiry packet in order to contact DCYF. You can also collaborate with private organizations to become licensed. These organizations focus primarily on children that require extra assistance and provide greater care. Foster care is just one of the many supports and services provided by organizations like those listed below. Look for "Individual Service Options" or "ISO" in the name. Here is a list of organizations and links to their foster care or ISO programs:

1. Waypoint
2. Network for Independent Services
3. Ascentria Care Alliance
4. Spaulding Youth Center
5. NFI North

Make contact with foster parent resources

Foster parents can find both official and unofficial supports to help make this trip a little more manageable. Social media helps parents connect, therefore I urge you to use it to make contact. All foster and adoptive parents are welcome at the New Hampshire Foster Adoptive Parent Association's (NHFAPA) quarterly meetings, which are held in 12 different sites throughout the state. These support groups are an excellent way to connect with organizations like Lynette Kaichen's Pass-Along Project, a non-profit that facilitates fast clothes delivery for children entering foster care. If this is a challenge you want to accept, look up the programs that are available for support in your state.

Side businesses as a career option

There are numerous reasons why side businesses are interesting, and for empty-nesters with more free time, now can be the ideal moment to investigate how this might work for you. You could be seeking for engaging new methods to fill the hole now that your family's spare time isn't being filled by activities revolving around your kids. You can pursue your passions, contribute your knowledge, learn new skills, make additional money, and test the waters for potential new jobs by engaging in side hustles (*Why Side Hustles Are Ideal for Empty Nesters*, 2019).

Here are a few suggestions to get your creative juices flowing:

Sell crafts (Etsy, Flea markets, consignment stores, crafty sales, fairs)

1. Buy and sell antiques
2. sell your photographs or your designs to Shutterfly
3. Become a tutor
4. Become a coach if you know a sport
5. If you know a 2nd language give classes
6. If you are musical- teach music lessons
7. Write a book through Kindle Direct Publishing
8. Babysit before and after school
9. If you make jewelry-sell it
10. Make practical things from junk (birdhouses-windchimes)
11. Become an Uber driver
12. Sell on eBay
13. Start a consignment store
14. Do a service to get the elderly their groceries, and medications, and take them to appointments
15. Do a dog walking/ dog sitting business
16. Clean homes
17. Weed gardens and maintain them
18. Join HireAChef to work as a personal chef.
19. Become a virtual assistant
20. Rent out your clothes on online platforms

Before beginning this chapter, you may have thought there's nothing much you are capable of offering to the world. I hope now you realize the sky is the limit, and the only thing holding you back from reaching your full capacity is you, yourself. When you feel down and demotivated, remind yourself to

> "Trust in the LORD with all your heart and
> lean not on your own understanding; in all
> your ways submit to him, and he will
> direct your path." – Proverb 3: 5-6

CHAPTER 6: LETTING GO SO THEY GROW

D o you remember the time you were transitioning from a kid into an adult? Every advice your parents offered made you irritable. The ages 18 to 20 are a difficult age. A lot of things are changing in your child's life. They are adapting to a new lifestyle, shouldering new responsibilities, struggling with getting good grades while maintaining a social life, and whatnot. And that's not hard to understand because we've all been there. Of course, it is difficult to stand back and learn not to help your children through the difficult situations they are in, as a result of the choices they made. You've been their guiding light forever, but you must hand the torch to them as they navigate their independent lives.

Good communication is key to keeping strong ties with your adult children. Plan occasional scheduled visits, face-to-face chats, emails, and letters to check in and speak to remain in touch. But remember, our advice is welcomed, ONLY when requested. It's also important to keep in mind that as their parents, you are the guests in their home - not the other way around.

If you are worried your adult children will get tired of you and remove you from their life, they probably will. But only when you try to dominate them or impose your parenting beliefs, anxieties, or ideals on them. It's important to give them the space to grow and make their own decisions, without constantly trying to control them or tell them what to do.

It can be difficult but is good to hold back on offering an opposing viewpoint about how we as parents believe they should live. Our children leave home for different reasons such as for college, new jobs, and the military. Needless to say, our love and support for them will never stop. However, it is our turn to let go and refrain from rushing to their aid. Let them learn through their own desires, choices, mistakes, and adult struggles, just like we did when we were growing up.

So, how do you let go while also building a strong relationship with them and remaining a part of their life? Let's find out!

Bonding with your adult children

To stay a part of your children's lives, there are a number of things you can do. However, when overridden with emotions, it can become hard to differentiate right from wrong. You may not know when you're crossing lines and invading their boundaries. So, here are some great ways you can utilize to begin building a healthy bond with your adult children.

Go on dates with them

We're all busy, and our schedules sometimes make it difficult to find time to see each other in person. That's why many parents opt to use texting and phone conversations to stay in touch with their adult children. While this is great, in-person contacts are equally essential. Parents who have the best ties with their adult children frequently communicate with them by text, phone call, and in-person interactions. In fact, those parents who had the closest relationships with their children were 1.5 times more likely to have frequent eye and physical contact (Larkin, 2018). Schedule a date & time on the calendar to meet up with your child(ren)

Create new rituals

Personalized family rituals have a special touch of their own. You don't have to stick to celebrating formal holidays to keep up with your family traditions. Come up with something that suits your adult children and you. Consider each other's interests and schedules, and form a yearly or bi-annual ritual to keep in touch during these special moments.

Help them paint and decorate their new home

It may be enjoyable as well as beneficial for a mother to assist her adult daughter or son in crossing off some of the items on their never-ending list of things to do. Visit with your painting garb on ready to roll up your sleeves, pitch in and make their dreams come true. Celebrate with pizza once the job is done.

Giving advice on interior design in terms of aesthetic appeal is one approach to this. They could require a new table, living room drapes, or fresh paint makeovers. You'll have achieved that ideal balance that so many parents struggle to reach if you can act as a rallying point without being overly opinionated. You can unload your home of extra furniture, sheets, dishes, pictures you no longer need by helping your child make their home a home.

Drop the embarrassing nicknames

Giving your children sweet nicknames when they were toddlers, such as chicklet, tatar-bud, baby cakes, gibby, giblet, doodles, and stinky-pants was acceptable. But now that they're grownups, they ought to be handled accordingly. If you keep using their baby names around them, they will never feel appreciated or like an adult around you. And that's exactly what you don't want them to feel. Our children have grown up therefore our interaction must also change. Treating them like you would any other adult will be appreciated if you want them to value your presence and company.

Get interested in their interests

Even if it's not something you often like doing, showing interest in the things your children enjoy shows them that you have an open mind, which they will admire. They could even repay the favor by going with you to an activity you like. And who knows if either one of you genuinely starts enjoying the activity?

Don't act desperate

Let your kids know you have an interesting life of

your own. Now, I'm not suggesting you stop talking to them, but it's good not to reply to their text messages the minute you receive them. When you don't, it can make you look a bit more fascinating to them. Be sure not to take their sporadic silence personally. Most essentially, keep in mind that if you want to establish a strong bond with your adult children, emotional dependence is a major no-no. Speak to your partner, a friend, or a counselor if you're having trouble adjusting to the empty nest or this new stage in your relationship with your children, but don't hold them accountable for your feelings; they already have enough on their plates as they attempt to live their new lives.

Spend one-on-one time!

To build a strong relationship with anyone in your life, it's important you spend one-on-one time with them, without the interference of another individual. This way, the conversations can revolve around just the two of you, and that may make you and your children feel a deeper connection.

Be receptive to feedback

It is important to be open to listening when it comes to building a strong relationship with your children (or anyone). Your children may become distant if they don't like some things you do, but can't speak to you about them because they fear you will become defensive. When living apart, such things should always be discussed to avoid misunderstandings and remain a part of each other's lives. Remember, your child is more likely to want to be close to you if you can demonstrate that you can take criticism well, are self-aware, and understand how they feel.

Letting go

While it is essential to build a strong bond with your children, it is more important to accept the fact that things are not going to be the same. Why is that so? Well, if you keep clinging on to how things used to be, you are much more likely to become over-indulgent in your children's lives. And as we already know, that's the last thing you should do. Also, you can't build great things unless you first build yourself. Oftentimes, we begin fixing broken relationships without fixing ourselves. The result? Everything shatters in the process.

Here are a few tips that can help you get started with the process of letting go (Army Mom Strong, 2021):

Have faith!

Multiple facets of faith exist. It might be both faith in God and confidence in your child's skills. As moms, we cling on tightly to our children when they leave because we are too afraid to let go. The constant worry about if they will be able to look after themselves and make it through the day eats at us. But it's not right to spend your days wallowing in emotions. Instead, allow God to take over and have faith in the abilities of your children and what you've taught them; that's really the only way to let go of your worries. In the words of Ann Landers, remember, "It is not what you do for your children, but what you have taught them to do for themselves, that will make them successful human beings." The scripture verse that comforted me was "Train up a child in the way he should go; even when he is old he will not depart from it." Proverbs 2:26

Focus on your own life

You already have numerous ways at your disposal to fix your life and start living it your way. (I mean, I dedicated a whole chapter to that!) Allow these temporary melancholic moments to pass, and then continue living the loving, peaceful life you deserve.

Keep in mind, life is an ever-evolving change and transition- it is that circle of life. We unintentionally did the same to our parents. Looking back we have a 20/20 vision. I was oblivious to my parents' pain when we all left home just as our children are oblivious to ours. Step back, let them grow into their new-found independent lives and we too can embrace our new-found (yet strange at first and then wonderful) life.

It's good to let go!

When you let old things go, you make the space for new and more fulfilling things to come to you. It is okay to feel hurt or sad, yet don't let that disrupt your journey of letting go. Become the best version of yourself that you can be! You are in charge of your emotions and ideas. What kind of mom adventure you have is entirely up to you.

Practicing great parenting

Nothing great comes without effort. You have made an effort to bring up your kids in the best way possible, and now you must make the effort to still be their parent, but in a different way. The roles you are used to playing will change; you may become a mother-in-law, grandmother, best friend, or counselor now. When my grandchildren came, I fit into my children's lives once again in a different way. Being invited to share in the milestones of my children's lives brings unspeakable joy. I learned that I will always be their parent, their biggest cheerleader, aside from God, the one they can call on in times of need, to request advice, or just talk. They were my world, then my world got crushed when they left, and now I have been invited to participate in their new worlds and it is a beautiful place to be.

Talk with your kids

Speculating is pointless. Ask your children what would make them happy regarding your presence in their lives. Listen to what they have to say but don't just do it for the sake of it; choose doable suggestions that you can implement in your life.

Mail a card or little gifts

While sending texts and meeting in person is always good, sometimes you can also gift your kids meaningful things to let them know that you are thinking of them. Don't opt for pricey or extravagant things since that's the only way to keep this gesture spontaneous and frequent. When my son was out on his own he asked me to write down the recipes he loved that I made for my family while growing up. I also baked up his favorite no bake chocolate-peanut butter cookies, sent his favorite cereals, a bag of skittles and mailed them as a surprise. All those little gestures are appreciated and reminders of the special bond that a mother has with her child. It was a nice way to make that fond connection and put a smile on your child's face.

Treat their spouses, girlfriends, and boyfriends with acceptance, respect, love, and support

Behave with their loved ones as though they were family. Don't think of them as your child's other half. Instead, consider them a part of your own family. This will help you do things for them from your heart. And you will never find out how much your child will appreciate you when you respect their choices until you actually do so.

Send them something you run across that you think they will love, laugh at or enjoy

Who doesn't enjoy funny videos or memes on the internet? Sharing with your children things you think they would be interested in is a great way to stay in touch with them and let them know you are thinking of them. Something as simple as a spice they cannot find on the shelves can be dropped in the mail and bring a smile.

Support their side jobs or businesses (personalized gifts)

Parents are usually very encouraging of their children's careers and business choices. However, the side hustles usually don't receive much appreciation since they are not full-time jobs, but more like passion projects. Showing support for your children's passions and helping them grow further is guaranteed to make them appreciate you in more ways than you can imagine.

Pray for them

Parenting never stops. Even when they are adults, eventually married with children, they will face challenges and our job is to support them by listening and praying for them. Pray that God directs their path and gives them wisdom and strength during challenging times. When you're not there, your prayers and God will always be.

Attend their gigs if they have them

In order to show them you are proud of what they're doing in life, attend their gigs and appreciate their work. It is always good to text kind words of encouragement to your children, but it's even better when you do it in person.

Give them space

Establish new roles, allow your children to make their decisions, give them their privacy, and allow them the time they need to nurture their interests and independence. Let them figure themselves out first before they realize the need for other people, like you, in their life. Remember, "a wise parent humors the desire for independent action, so as to become the friend and advisor when his absolute rule shall cease." —Elizabeth Gaskell

Managing Aging Parents and College-going Kids

Some of us have more than just the stress of an empty nest to deal with. When your aging parents are living with you, you must ensure your empty nest phase doesn't affect them negatively.

Stress reduction is mostly a function of preparation. Make sure your kid has the necessary skills to take care of himself or herself, including the ability to do laundry, shop, comprehend a budget, prepare meals or have a meal plan, locate medical treatment, possess medical identification, and even have a supply of over-the-counter medications (*Empty Nesters: Coping With Aging Parents & College-Bound Kids*, n.d.).

On the other hand, be as prepared as you can for aging parents, and make sure that all necessary arrangements have been done for the unexpected future. You can relieve stress by providing for your child and elderly parents in the ways mentioned above.

CHAPTER 7: A FLAME, FLICKER OR SMOKE

Life is more fun when you share it with friends. If you are married and your marriage has been neglected and barely hanging on by a thread, rekindle that flame. You loved each other once before, you can fall in love again. Restart your dating life and look for activities you two can enjoy together. Start expressing to one another what you value, adore, and are grateful for about them. You'll stay away from the suffering, shame, and unforeseen consequences that come with divorce. If you are divorced, you will deal with the fallout from your broken marriage that your kids suffer as well as concerns related to divorce. For the sake of your children and grandkids, it is preferable to work toward moving past your marriage's dissolution and obtaining an amicable divorce. For the sake of your children and grandkids, you must throw down the sword, be merciful to one another, let go, make amends, become friends, and be able to spend holidays with your ex, his new spouse, or close companion if possible. Dating might be a little difficult, but now is the time to do it and make new connections and partnerships. It's time to let go of your guilt and realize that parents are first and foremost imperfect people before they transform into superheroes, obnoxious enforcers, and lastly, friends to their grown children.

Fixing your marriage

Enroll in an online marriage retreat program and explore marriage fitness with Mort Fertel online counseling for example. If you or your spouse have recently told the other, "I love you, but I am not in love with you," there's clearly a big problem at hand that you both need to find a way around.

While it may appear that you are just differentiating between "various loves," in reality, you are expressing your uncertainty about what love actually is. You basically mean to say, "I care about you, but you no longer excite me" (Fertel, n.d.).

And as a result, you both may suffer from marital issues, which may then make you reconsider if you even married the right person, to begin with.

Well, the truth is all relationships go through a similar cycle. You at first fell in love with your husband. You looked forward to their call, desired their touch, and enjoyed their quirkiness. It wasn't difficult to fall in love with your spouse. In actuality, the encounter was wholly unplanned. You didn't need to take any action.

Being in love is simple. It's a passive, unplanned encounter.

Fertel (n.d.) explains that the joy of love wears off after a few years of marriage. It is a part of EVERY relationship's natural cycle. Phone calls start to worry you, contact is not always appreciated, and your spouse's quirks begin to drive you crazy rather than make you laugh.

Every relationship will experience this period differently, but if you reflect on your marriage, you'll see a marked contrast between the first phase when you were in love and the later, duller or even furious time.

And when you and your partner recall the bliss of the love you previously shared, you may start yearning for that encounter with someone else. Marriages fail at this point. People go outside their marriage for fulfillment and blame their partner for their misery.

You may now begin to wonder, how do I get my spouse to change?

The thing about change is that by nature, we are resistant to change that is forced upon us, not change that occurs on its own (Fertel, n.d.). So, with the change that we initiate, we have no issues. However, we struggle mightily to change when we feel pressured or coerced to do something.

Although your spouse may not be ready to make a change today for the benefit of your marriage, this does not mean they do not want you to have a happy marriage. Everyone desires a successful marriage. Instead, it's because they want the change to be their own thing if they're going to make it, not something you have asked them to do (Fertel, n.d.).

The solution to this problem can come from you changing yourself first. In turn, you could serve as an inspiration for your spouse to change. There's no harm in taking the first step on the road to recovery if it can end as a win-win situation for both of you!

The first and most significant change can come from giving up the desire to be right in every argument. Those silent treatments you give each other to prove a point only worsen things. You have most likely felt that heaviness in your chest when you and your partner aren't speaking to each other. You both know it's not right, but you both won't end it until you're proven right.

However, marriages don't work that way. When you start seeing your relationship as everything, you'll realize that being right is meaningless in your marriage. The choice is yours to make. Does your desire to be correct outweigh your desire for a fulfilling marriage? I hope not!

Secondly, if you're used to giving your spouse ultimatums to fix themselves or their habits, trust me, that won't work! Giving your partner a deadline to fix their mess will create clear ground rules for your marriage (Fertel, n.d.). You'll establish limits and restrictions, which is basically what you're hoping to do.

But where will your spouse get the motivation to follow the rules you've set? They won't.

Your partner is aware of the error in their ways.

They know in their hearts that their actions are unethical and they are ruining your marriage, even if they won't say it or try to defend it. The actual issue isn't them acknowledging they are wrong. Instead, it is that they don't care and lack the motivation to act morally.

Your partner must be willing to stop. Their internal drive is the crucial factor here. An ultimatum imposes regulations from the outside; it says nothing about the inside's lack of drive.

So, how can you influence their internal motivation, then? Connecting with them is the key. When the connection you build with them takes over, the void in their life they fill through other ways will automatically be filled up by you.

Invest time and patience in restoring your marriage. Each person needs to concentrate on improving themselves, as both parties must accept responsibility for the breakdown of their marriage (Fertel, n.d.).

It's that simple!

Baby Steps to Healing a Failed Marriage

So, you have decided you want to keep your union together. Good; you are aware of your goals. The only issue now is how you will repair your marriage.

First, let's get one thing straight. The exchange of a few words cannot resolve a problem that started due to action; you must take action to reverse it now.

You may wonder, "what actions?"

Advice from Mort Fertel , a nice remark and a tender touch are the first baby steps in salvaging a broken marriage. Fertel (n.d.) suggests the following actions:

A "**talk charge**" is a 60-second, positive conversation with your spouse that is NOT about a logical issue. It's a lighthearted conversation. Additionally, you don't require your spouse's support. If needed, you speak, and they take note. Even a voicemail can be useful.

Similar to a talking charge, a **touch charge** operates by contact. It is a tender physical touch you give your partner, warm enough to establish a connection at that particular time; it's not foreplay or an attempt to make love.

Remember, your marriage cannot be saved by a single incident. You cannot give a present, do a favor, send flowers or write a letter to fix it. There is no magic bullet. There isn't a single thing you can do or say to make things better. You've been in this mess for years, and it will take time for you to come out.

Marriages that were failing once ultimately thrived when at least one partner made a long-term commitment to doing great, small things. Creating the right habits and practicing them repeatedly is what will help you. Consistency is key here, so don't give up, no matter how redundant your efforts may sometimes feel in the moment.

If you have any second thoughts about these tips by Mort Fertel working out, here are some reviews that will strengthen your belief in them and in your ability to bring about much-needed changes in your marriage.

1. "Best money I've spent. My wife was totally against it and wanted nothing to do with me. So I did it myself, and after a few days, she gave in and gave it a try. I must say it opened both of our eyes and we are doing better than ever. We definitely still need work, but your techniques definitely have us going in the right direction. I believe I can definitely say it's a success story even though it's only been 3 weeks. We talk, laugh, and have fun again. Thanks again and I definitely recommend it to anyone that was in my situation." -Pete Llamas

2. "I started on the Lone Ranger Track. Here's a person who didn't want to talk to me 2 weeks ago but now wants to spend every single possible moment. It doesn't take 2 people to save the marriage." -Eric Cole

3. "I was in the lone ranger track, totally on my own. It was the darkest time of my life. But I was encouraged by Mort's message that one person can save a marriage because you always hear 'it takes two' and my husband was not interested. Ultimately, I changed so much that my husband noticed and asked what was causing the changes and I told him, Mort Fertel. He agreed to listen to the tapes and do the workbook, and ultimately he went to a therapist, which for my husband was a miracle...our marriage is better than it was

before…because of Mort's help." -Heather Powers

If you're still all over the place, not knowing what direction to go in with your marriage, you can employ The 7 Secrets to Fixing Your Marriage by Mort Fertel. It's absolutely free!

Seven Ingredients for a Successful Relationship

Every relationship differs in how it defines itself successfully. You may believe a partnership free from strife is the best kind, while others may consider having endless fun, being really close to someone, or laughing a lot is ideal. Whatever definition you choose, it outlines your requirements and wishes for a happy married life.

However, regardless of your definition of the ideal type, the following seven ingredients are essential for ANY successful relationship (Kaiser, 2016):

1. **Respect**

Respect is the cornerstone of any strong relationship. It entails having consideration for your partner's needs and wishes and behaving or speaking with them in mind at all times. It is expected that your spouse will adhere to the same rules. Respect is treating the person you're with the same amount of consideration you would give to your own comfort, pleasure, and well-being.

2. **Loyalty**

We are joyful when we are confident that someone is watching out for us. Relationships work best when both parties are dedicated to continuously supporting one another. This implies that if your spouse is being irritated by someone, you will either support them directly or indirectly. This also implies that you should never discuss a problem with your spouse in front of others if you feel that they have done anything that is improper or that you disapprove of.

3. Priority

Let your spouse know they are a priority if you want a stronger, more fulfilling connection. Spend time and effort communicating with each other and attending to their needs and wants. Make sure the two of you spend "quality time" together alone so that you can bond and appreciate each other's company. Finding a balance can help ensure that your relationship is not ignored, despite the importance of your job, children, and other duties.

4. Choose your battles

Couples who are truly happy and healthy to know when to discuss difficulties and leave them alone. Let things go if you can while still enjoying your spouse. Bring up a subject if you find it difficult to forget it and dwell on it often. When you bring it up, be sure to do so calmly, in private, and when it is convenient for you two to talk about it. Never discuss anything distressing in bed or in front of kids, relatives, or friends.

If your spouse is touchy about certain topics, you want to be careful not to offend them when addressing such subjects. You are more likely to get an amicable reaction and address the problem if you gently approach the subject. And that's what you want, right?

5. Loving gestures

In terms of interpersonal interactions, the adage "Actions speak louder than words" is crucial. You must act on your feelings of love for someone in addition to just feeling that way. Use nice language, show physical affection, and scatter small love notes about the house. Make sure you express your love to your spouse in no uncertain terms, whether through a verbal or material gesture.

6. Put in the work

Successful partners are aware that maintaining a positive dynamic requires effort on both sides. Work together with the chores around the house. That implies that there are times when you must do things you do not want to do because they are important to your relationship. Other times, it requires making the additional effort to control your emotions or pay attention to your partner's worries, even if doing so isn't the most straightforward or convenient course of action at the time. If a relationship is to be effective, pleasant, and long-lasting, it requires a lot of work.

7. Focus on the positives

Even the strongest partnerships can face difficulties, and even the most lovely couples can experience less-than-ideal times. Those looking for a good relationship will counter the bad with a positive one when circumstances are rough. If your partner is cranky after a hard day, think about your enjoyable weekend or how hilarious your partner can usually be. Focus on the fact that your spouse is a fantastic father or a great cook if you've noticed that they're a little untidy, for instance, and it doesn't appear to be changing. Reverse your thoughts to affirm that your partner is wonderful and that you are content to be together.

Your journey to fixing your marriage could be at any stage. Some may not have to worry about working on the fundamentals of their marriage, while others may have to redo it all over again. Wherever you may be in your marriage, you can always rekindle the romance between the two of you and find more than you may think there is to your relationship. Many times, we come to believe that romance was just a phase that has ended now. However, not a single successful marriage exists without romance.

Here are some ways you can reignite the fire of romance in your empty-nester relationship (Eagle Family, 2017):

Invest in yourself

You have put time and effort into investing in your kids; now, invest in yourself. Both individually and together, try out new ideas. Discovering new interests gives your life and your relationship some excitement. Make a list of the activities you enjoy doing and the dreams you have for the future.

Talk to your spouse about the items on the list after it is complete. Create a comprehensive list of everything you wish to accomplish as a couple, and do all of them. Watch how it excites both of your lives.

Talk about yourself and each other

Many couples talk about children or family issues more when they have kids. They don't talk as much as lovers do.

You two were lovers before getting married. Conversations throughout the dating stage were very different from those during the child-bearing years. Go back to when you used to spend hours interacting with one another.

Talk about your aspirations and worries. A greater understanding of your partner is advisable. A lot has changed since the day you fell in love, keep it in mind. Intimacy may be gained through communication. Being intimate allows for the rekindling of romantic feelings.

Create a honeymoon at home

Do you recall how frequently you cuddled and kissed before having children? Why not plan a second honeymoon with the time you have available?

Some couples claim that their libido declines with age. However, having an empty nest may help you out there. It fuels the fire as husband and wife spend more time together and develop their connection. Profit from having the place to yourselves once more. Rekindle love and have delicious romantic dinners.

Go on dates

Many couples believe that when their children have gone out, date nights become less crucial since you can finally focus on your partner practically constantly without the interference of kids at home. However, being an empty nester doesn't automatically imply you can stop going on dates, which is a frequent misperception.

In fact, this could not be further from the truth! Spending time with your spouse on a regular basis should always be a top priority. Remember, "There is only one happiness in this life, to love and be loved." — George Sand.

It can be difficult to plan dates initially since you've been out of practice for so long. If you're looking for ways to make your date nights unique, try these ones out by Macey (2022):

Dance away!

A terrific method to bond with one another is via dancing. Nothing compares to laughing a lot, listening to great music, and being held by your special someone. It doesn't matter if you don't know how to dance, just focus on living the moment to the fullest. In fact, you could also go to a weekly dance class together.

See a brand-new film at a theatre.

When was the last time you went to a freshly released movie unaccompanied by your children? Now that you don't have to stress about getting home in time to pick up a babysitter, organize your evening around watching a movie at your preferred cinema with your partner. You could even pick a theatre far from your house and incorporate a long drive into your date night.

Go on a date to the supermarket!

Consider giving each of you the opportunity to select an appetizer, a main meal, and a side dish or dessert. Don't discuss your plans with one another! Go to the grocery shop, break apart, and get everything you require. Get cooking when you get home! Once everything is finished, you'll have everything you need for a four-course meal ready, AND you'll have created a lovely surprise for your beloved!

Visit a nearby food truck for supper!

Even better, try a different food truck for each course of your dinner, in any sequence! Take advantage of the first food truck you see that has sweets. Just make sure every dish you eat is from a brand-new truck! You might just find some delicious underrated food you could also enjoy later.

Go shopping!

For your date night, go shopping. Each of you gets $10 to $20 to spend on the other to make it more enjoyable. Visit your favorite retailer separately and surprise your special someone with their favorite goods. It will be so much fun to see what ideas your partner has! Maybe you will even find likes and dislikes they have developed over time that you weren't aware of.

You could also try out these ideas by Eagle Family (2019):

1. Go on a picnic at a new location.

2. Rotate who tries new restaurant recommendations.
3. Play a round of golf together.
4. Recall your first date in detail. Create it again.
5. Travel together for a day.
6. Go fly kites at the seashore.
7. Pick fruit together.
8. Go on walks together.
9. Watch the sun rising and setting.
10. Hold hands. How soon it begins to seem like a date will surprise you.
11. Check out cheese and jelly shops and sample everything.
12. Bake something together.
13. With the intention of buying gifts for one another, visits a thrift shop with your spouse. The one with the most intriguing selection wins!
14. Visit bike paths and go for a ride.
15. Take a vacation
16. Dance in the rain.
17. Browse wedding photo albums and watch movies together.
18. Visit the drive-in.
19. Play dating games to get to know each other better while having romantic date nights.

However, sometimes things just aren't meant to be. Despite making many efforts to save your marriage, you may end up realizing the differences are irreconcilable and it's best to go your separate ways. Or maybe you had known that all along but were looking for a better time to break things off. Whatever your situation may be, grey divorces (divorce in the later years) can be extremely tough. You've lived your entire life with one person, so letting them go is going to be difficult inevitably.

At this stage, you may be willing to try and save your marriage one last time before letting go. If all else fails, couples therapy could help you and your partner bridge the gaps that may be the reason behind your problems.

One may wonder, why couples divorce when the pressure of raising kids has finally been lifted. Isn't this the ideal time to enjoy life together? While it may appear that way, there is frequently much more going on in a relationship or with a particular person than is initially apparent when it comes to empty nesters and divorce (Dillon, n.d.).

These are the most common reasons for empty nest divorce (Dillon, n.d.):

1. An unsteady union.
2. Long-term marital neglect.

3. They put up with problems or attend counseling for years, yet they continue to be together for the kids.

4. Different perspectives on the empty nest and a lack of sympathy for the hurting spouse.

5. One partner's unwillingness to "let go" leads to marital issues

6. The primary caregiver becomes anonymous.

7. Age-related problems: for men, low testosterone; for women, hormonal changes that lower sex desire and energy.

8. Stress and irritation might result from being pushed into retirement or losing fulfilling work.

9. Financial strain is brought on by aging parents and adult offspring who "boomerang" and return home.

10. Boredom and having too much free time.

Coping with Divorce

No matter the reason for divorce, it may completely upend your reality, making it challenging to get through the workday and remain productive. However, you may take steps to ease this challenging adjustment (*Coping With Separation And Divorce*, n.d.):

1. **Recognize that it's acceptable to experience diverse emotions.** It's common to experience strong emotions, including sadness, rage, exhaustion, frustration, and confusion. You

can possibly experience future anxiety.
Recognize that such responses will wane with
time. Going into the unknown is daunting,
even if the marriage was dysfunctional.

2. **Take a break for yourself.** For a while, give
yourself permission to experience and
perform less than optimally. For a period, you
might not be able to care for others exactly
the way you're used to or be as effective at
work. Take some time to recover, reorganize,
and regain your energy.

3. **Don't suffer alone.** You might find it helpful
to talk to your loved ones about your
sentiments during this time. Consider
attending a support group so you can interact
with people going through similar things.
Your stress levels will go up if you isolate
yourself, and your focus will suffer. Your
career, relationships, and general health will
also suffer. Never hesitate to ask for outside
assistance if you need it.

4. **Take care of yourself and your emotional
needs.** Take care of your body and yourself.
Spend some time relaxing, eating healthy, and
exercising. Try to stick as closely as you can
to your regular habits. Avoid making
important choices or altering your life's goals.
Avoid using drugs, alcohol, or cigarettes as a
coping mechanism since they simply make
things worse.

5. **Refrain from arguing and engaging in power conflicts with your spouse or ex-spouse.** If an argument breaks out during a conversation, politely propose that you both try discussing again later and then get up and leave the room or hang up the phone.

6. **Spend some time pursuing your hobbies.** Get back into activities you like doing alone or without your partner. Have you always wanted to learn how to paint or join a softball team for intramural play? Enroll in a class, devote time to your interests, volunteer, and enjoy life by meeting new people.

7. **Remain optimistic.** Finding new hobbies and friends, as well as moving on with realistic expectations, will help you through this transition even if things might not be the same. Be adaptable. Family traditions will still be vital if you have children, but some of them might need to be modified. Aid in developing fresh family activities.

8. **Read books.** Books on grey divorce can help you cope with this phase of your life. "Gray Divorce: What We Lose and Gain from Mid-Life Splits" is a great read if you're looking for suggestions to read. It discusses optimistic outlooks and essential supporting government policies that may be implemented for those recently divorced.

If things get tough between you and your partner, get a mediator to help rifle through keeping the house, downsizing for when college kids come home, alimony for long-term marriages/support for the spouse who is impacted financially and splitting assets and debts fairly. Having an amicable divorce for the kid's and grandchildren's sake is the best way to go about it. You don't want to drive your kids away from you over disputes with your ex-partner.

Forgiving your ex-partner and fully letting go is essential, no matter the differences between you two. Holding grudges in your heart will eat away your sanity and won't do you any good. I heard it said, it actually is like drinking poison and thinking it will not hurt you.

In the end, just know that life will return to normal, albeit "normal" might not be what you had anticipated. Remember,

"Weeping may endure for the night but joy comes in the morning." – Psalm: 30:5

CHAPTER 8: SPECIAL OCCASIONS

Remember that time you didn't have a single minute on your hands during the holidays? The house was overflowing with beds, noise, and youngsters celebrating the spirit of Christmas while you were basking in the joy of having the whole family together, attending to chore after chore so everyone could have a good time.

Of course, change is never easy and this year, you have none of that hustle and bustle to deal with. Thoughts of sadness and this Christmas will be a gloomy, lonely, dull, and boring can easily creep into your head.

Yes, the kids won't be spending Christmas at home but does that mean you can't have a good one now? What about all those years you celebrated Christmas when your kids weren't part of the world? When unwelcome ideas of an empty nest invade, it's important to focus on the good and change negative mindsets.

Understanding that the kids not being home doesn't mean they don't love you is key to surviving through the empty nest holiday season.

Here are some survival strategies by Tibbetts (2022) to get you through this phase:

Decorate for zoom!

Instead of decorating for kids to gather around the Christmas tree, change the decor to suit whatever will look best on the zoom calls you to make to your loved ones. Think about where it would be best to put lighting with respect to the computer camera, given that lighting to the side makes you seem better on a Zoom square than overhead lights. Consider working on the background with special and beloved Christmas objects for online meetings during the coming months.

The Why-Decorate-Blues may be brought on by empty nests, but online life may also bring on fresh vigor as you discover tech-savvy methods to share and appreciate classic goods with the people you love.

Cook together but in a different way.

Grandchildren who are staying elsewhere should still have the opportunity to bake cookies with Grandma. A regular Zoom or a lengthy Facetime may have both households cooking the same family food if their kitchen and yours were prepared beforehand. You may show them how to prepare all of your wonderful Christmas recipes, as well as perhaps a few brand-new ones.

Don't anticipate flawless camera angles. This type of interaction calls for movement, such as the jiggling of a phone, tablet, or laptop when the cooking activity varies.

Read your favorite books.

Christmas novels are important. Reading vacation novels together over Zoom or Facetime also works, though it's not quite as enjoyable as cuddling. If the grandkids aren't too young, taking turns could be a great way to indulge in this.

Prepare the table!

One of the best empty nest survival advice is to look after yourself. The nicest holiday customs still hold a significant position of eating at the table even during the empty nest. I have a friend who hosted what he called Christmas dinner for the misfit guys and gals or for the single, widowed or divorced friends. Giving "misfit gifts" during a gift swap can bring much humor and laughter. Being alone during the holidays need not be depressing.

Consider using traditional holiday dishes while setting the table as an empty nest survival strategy. Of course, that also necessitates the resolve to enjoy and be grateful as you have your meal alone or with friends.

Modify how you serve holiday favorites. Perhaps now is the time to discover delicious new delicacies to send to their homes. Send a nice gift to yourself at the empty nest address as well.

Could the introduction of sweets from a renowned chocolatier help to bridge that distance? Or salmon taken in the wild? Or the finest collection of jellies ever? You could pass on family traditions and write down the recipes of holiday favorites that you and your children became accustomed while growing up in your home. The list is endless.

Volunteer To Alleviate Loneliness of Empty Nest.

To avoid the sadness and fill the void left by the realization that no one is coming home for the holidays there are some things you can do.

To fill the gaps as holiday customs and circumstances change, numerous community service options need to be floated. You can volunteer to serve Christmas dinner at a neighborhood shelter or pay a visit to a nursing home on Christmas Day if you don't want to spend the holiday season alone. You could brighten someone else's day and possibly win a new friend. Your community is home to many fantastic nonprofits that could use your assistance during and after the holidays.

Holiday preparations done differently.

Since you don't have to worry about preparing beds, towels, and food for houseguests, perhaps the silver lining is how much more deliberate time you can now dedicate to selecting the elusive right gifts. Do gifts need to be shipped far in advance if no one is coming home for the holidays? Plan ahead, wrap and ship early. You can even go shop for yourself and put gifts under the tree addressed to you from Santa! Why not?

Enjoy yourself.

This holiday, unclaimed time and space may portend a year full of fresh books to read, films to watch, and musical compositions to hear. You could even change the affliction of nobody visiting by asking friends to come over. It all depends on what your definition of enjoyment is.

Apart from Christmas, other holiday gatherings could be rotated among the children's houses (Thanksgiving at one child's home, Christmas at another, and plans for Easter and the Fourth of July at another). Send cards to your adult children celebrating every holiday complete with little gift bags. If you have grandchildren you might send holiday specific books, coloring books, little holiday crafts, and cute cake or cookie decorating recipes complete with cookie cutters that would add cheer to their holiday. Don't forget Valentine's Day, Saint Patrick's Day, Hanukkah and any other holiday you may celebrate. After the holidays, there are always clearance sales where you can stock up for future gag gifts without breaking the bank. It is fun to be a giver and sprinkle cheer when you can. I personally get much joy anticipating the happiness felt from my unexpected gestures of mailing out love and kindness.

Don't forget to pat yourself on the back for pulling through such a difficult phase of your life. I assure you, once this is over, beautiful things await!

Visit them.

Your kids most likely have jobs, which means they have limited vacation time that they may want to utilize in a way that you haven't thought about. Knowing how long to remain is tough if you leave the nest and visit the kids. Thus, attempt to think of a strategy to have a shorter visit yet a lengthy vacation. Look for other things to do in the region. There are several destinations that specialize in literary excursions. You may satisfy your want to get away by taking a side trip without staying too long with the kids.

Additionally, you could book a B&B near their house to allow them space and privacy while also being able to visit them.

CHAPTER 9: LIVING THE DREAM

I t is time to clean out the attics, basement, closets, drawers, and bedrooms, redecorate, open the windows, let the sunlight in, and plant that garden. It sounds like a lot of things to do at once, but when you take it one thing at a time, you'll see it's really not that hard.

Indeed, the process of purging and letting go is a hard one, but better things can't come your way if you keep holding on to the ones you don't need any longer. I know that's easier said than done. I bawled like a baby going through dusty keepsakes in the attic and basement. It is funny how the kids leave trophies, favorite childhood toys, and memoirs behind for us to wrestle with what to do with them. Fill one box with mementos for each kid, one box with items to sell or give away, and one box marked garbage.

With this new space, you create, make spare guest

rooms, a new office, a huge bathroom with a jacuzzi, change a room into a huge walk-in closet or downsize and sell. It's time to remodel your house to accommodate YOUR new way of living as you embark on this new phase of your life.

Let's begin!

Decluttering your space

From those cartoon curtains in your bathroom to the drawn-on walls in your living room, your house is a bunch of things that represent your children at different stages of their life. But decluttering to help yourself out of this emotional stage in life is important.

In fact, your life will run more easily if your home is organized since you won't have to set out on the journey to seek and search for items all the time, helping you not only create cleaner spaces, but also a clearer mind. You'll probably start to feel the impulse to start planning your days more effectively after you start becoming organized around the house.

Here are some easy strategies for decluttering any space in your house quickly and easily (Jane, n.d.):

Start with the space that will make you feel the happiest.

The biggest challenge in decluttering a room is deciding where to start. So, it is wise to start with the area that would provide you with the most value for your time.

For most, this could be the kitchen since it is simple to divide into small portions, such as one drawer or one cupboard at a time. Simply turn on some music, promise yourself to stop when you don't feel like doing more, and start right away!

Taking baby steps

The key to getting started is to divide up difficult jobs into smaller, more doable ones before beginning with the first one.

The best strategy for tackling something that appears intimidating is to accomplish it in little chunks. Small, manageable tasks are always less intimidating than trying to complete a job all at once rather than bouncing from one unfinished task to the next. With this approach, you'll witness yourself getting a lot more done than you aimed as you'll get started sooner than later.

Divide your belongings into three stacks.

To begin with, be certain you have an adequate supply of trash bags or boxes for the stuff you're discarding. Create a space where goods may be placed for sale or donation, and keep boxes or bags available for such items as well.

Thoroughly clean the closet, cupboard, or drawer you're working on. After that, divide each item into three categories: items to retain, items to discard, and items to give away or sell.

It might be difficult to decide what to retain and what to donate at first, but it gets simpler as you progress. To be as happy as possible, you must decide what is most essential to you and what you can live without.

Find inventive ways to store what is left.

After that, neatly store anything that is left. By the time you reach this stage, you could discover that you need drawer trays, baskets, bins, or even just some folders and labels to help you arrange your belongings.

Search for aisles of simple and lovely storage options for your kitchen, bathroom, closets, workplace, and garage at nearby furniture stores. You're ought to find some great pieces.

Reconsider how you utilize your spaces.

By making better use of your space, you are better able to enhance your storage capacity and reduce clutter. Come up with innovative solutions to prevent stocking up more clutter in the future while still having your home look beautiful. One way you can do this is by having open cabinets or shelves in your kitchen. This way, you won't be able to gather useless material that you otherwise would in a closed cabinet.

Organize a garage sale.

Your attic or basement can hold great treasures which you put there once but may have completely forgotten about over the years. Make sure to rummage through them, then conduct a garage sale to sell all the treasures you've found there and around your house.

KonMari Method of Decluttering by Marie Kondo.

Marie Kondo, a Japanese cleaning advisor and author of the bestselling book, "The Life-Changing

Magic of Tidying Up," introduced a ground-breaking concept for decluttering with a track record of customers who never reverted to their former hoarding behaviors. The KonMari Method is her minimalistic method for organizing your belongings so that you focus on categories rather than individual rooms. The first six basic guidelines are as follows (Garrity, 2019):

1. Make a commitment to cleaning up.
2. Think of the lifestyle you desire.
3. First, finish the trashing. Give each object a genuine thank you for performing its purpose before discarding it.
4. Tidy by category then by location.
5. Observe the proper sequence.
6. Consider whether it makes you happy.

And there are five categories to work through:

1. Clothes
2. Books
3. Papers
4. Komono (a.k.a. Miscellaneous Items)
5. Sentimental Things

Although many people equate her technique with housekeeping, it truly focuses on getting rid of things that aren't useful. Kondo instructs you to start by clearing everything out of your closets and drawers, all the books from your shelves, and all the papers from your desk and storage bins, and so on. When you have a large pile, look over each thing and ask yourself if it makes you happy.

You should have a considerably smaller collection of stuff left after getting rid of everything in each category, which you can then put back in various cupboards, drawers, shelves, and boxes. Keep in mind that you must complete one category before going on to the next.

Downsize!

While you're on the journey of getting rid of unneeded things in your home, why not consider downsizing if you have extra space you don't require anymore? A big house can also feel emptier and more lonely than a smaller one. However, think it through thoroughly before going on with a decision.

The Empty Nest's decorations!

So, what do you do now with all that freed-up space in your house? Chances are you'll face a lot of indecisiveness at this point in your decluttering endeavor. Here are some tips by Gish (2018) to help you advance through this next stage of organizing your place:

Furniture shopping!

You are now free to purchase white or beige furniture that nobody will damage a week after you bring it home. Consider purchasing customized furniture. It's an excellent technique to make sure your items survive a long time and look beautiful.

One great recommendation is to begin in your bedroom since it can be one of the spaces your kids didn't spend a lot of time in. Even though you spend a lot of time there, it's doubtful that you've decorated it exactly as you'd like. Consider how the area where you read, dress, and sleep may better suit your requirements.

Put down fresh carpeting or flooring.

Even if your flooring is still in good repair, it could be worthwhile to replace it. After all, installing a new sort of flooring will greatly revitalize your house, and you won't have to worry about purchasing specific kinds of carpeting or flooring that are appropriate for children. Do you still have in mind the marble, natural stone, or mosaic tile you've always wanted to install? Well, what are you waiting for then?

Improve or Expand Your Entertainment Area.

Whether you choose to host big or small gatherings, you now have the possibility to reconsider your entertainment strategy. If you wanted to create a wine cellar instead of a gaming room in the basement, you might renovate the space to incorporate restored vintage pool tables. Consider adding barstools to your kitchen island or extra guest seating for your deck or patio to increase your entertainment space.

Refresh the exterior.

If you have a yard, there are a lot of fun things you can do with it, such as

- including a garden.
- offering a treehouse or play set for sale.
- building a pond.

- constructing a deck or screen porch.
- purchasing outdoor furniture.
- rebuilding your yard from the ground up.
- constructing a fountain
- using nice details such as string lights while decorating.
- building pathways with the pavement.
- turning your shed into a "he shed/she shed", a pool cabana, a dry sauna or a newly organized functional shed.

Even better, you could create an outdoor kitchen with sinks, grills, and other amenities. This may be a fun way to spice up your gathering options!

Throw yourself a party!

It is finally time to celebrate yourself. You've sacrificed your life to give your children the wings they now have. And you proved to be the strong person you are, making it out of the empty nest syndrome no matter how badly circumstances may have pulled you down. So, crack open the champagne and toast that YOU survived and thrived through one of the most difficult transitions of your life. You deserve it!

Thinking of ways to celebrate? Scott (2019) can help you out with that!

Prioritize your needs (and those of your partner).

Whatever you believe is appropriate for who you are might be the theme of the party. It's up to you whether that's a wild party or a calm dinner gathering. If you've lived through the empty nest as a couple (or as single), the celebration can even have a humorous theme, such as "finally married - without kids" or "still standing-without kids." You two are the true guests at the celebration.

Get the drinks ready.

It need not be alcoholic beverages. You may create some lovely mixed cocktails without alcohol. There are great mock-tail recipes that are delicious and festive or just serve wine and beer. This evening is yours to plan and decide.

You and your companion can offer as many beverages as you like, or you can even ask friends to bring them over.

Theme the Party as You Please.

Are you organized? Did you like organizing parties and birthdays for your kids? Even if you didn't, the prospect of throwing the perfect party is intriguing, isn't it? The party theme may be as straightforward or as intricate as you choose.

Go nuts; there is a ton of event planning options available both locally and online. You can have a massive boombox at your party for karaoke or hire a live band or comedian if you want. Possibly put out a disco ball, thematic decorations, light the fire pit and enjoy the company of friends and neighbors. The possibilities are endless.

Your bedtime is yours to decide!

Since it's your party, you may decide how long or how short it will last. You are free to ask guests to leave early. However, it's your life if you want a party that runs into the wee hours, have a blast. Nothing needs to be planned. Simply follow the ambiance of the evening and determine when to call it a night.

You could even make the event an overnight filling up those newly decorated guest bedrooms if you so desire. Your power has no boundaries (read: kids).

So, what are you waiting for? Get planning!

CONCLUSION

The empty nest takes you through your unexpected journey of unwanted but necessary changes in this life stage. You become aware of who you are and reflect on your wants, needs, and desires now that your child-rearing days are done. It is a phase in life that forces you to make decisions to reshape your identity, find your new purpose, rekindle relationships, hobbies, and interests and find happiness once again. It is a time to dig deep through layers of unresolved emotions, an array of life challenges, and unspoken fears. You are not alone in your travels as others have gone before you.

I have left a trail of things I learned along the way, suggestions to apply, ideas to survive, and new perspectives about yourself and others as you navigate your own challenges during this heart-wrenching period that can paralyze you if you let it. This is your survival guide, full of practical advice to walk you through to the other side so you can thrive and find your happiness once again. There is no time better to begin your transformation than now. You will no longer feel stuck, devastated, lonely, and worthless. You will become an empowered, happy person with value and purpose.

Be prepared to focus on the good, the bad, and the ugly. Roll up your sleeves, work consistently on your situations, and invest time to see positive change in your life. I salute the new you and your future success!

If you like this book please leave a review on Amazon. Your reviews are important and will help people find me so I can help others during this difficult stage in their life. May you find your way filled with blessings, happiness and fulfillment along this journey, called life. Live it well, my friend and celebrate the remarkable transformation of YOU!

ABOUT THE AUTHOR

Pamela Fariole is a teacher and mother, and the author of *How to Survive the Empty Nest Phase.*

Her work is aimed at parents coming to the end of their journey as caretakers for their children, helping them to adjust to life with an empty nest.

Pamela has three grown-up children who all live away from home and are focused on their careers. As a single parent, she found the empty nest phase extremely challenging and struggled with feelings of overwhelm, anxiety, and depression. She had been married for 33 years, and suddenly finding herself in an empty house, she realized she needed to find her purpose in order to rediscover her sense of self and set out on a path toward a happy future.

Pamela is a certified teacher, but no longer works in public school, instead tutoring children online. This, alongside her writing, gives her the purpose and financial security she had been seeking. She is determined to help other people in her position find joy as they adjust to a more independent life after their children leave home.

Pamela has three grandchildren and a fourth on the way, and loves spending time with them. When she's not with her family, she enjoys spending the weekends with her friends and visiting new places. She loves music, her flower gardens, and good food. She finds joy in the world all around her and is always looking forward to her next adventure.

REFERENCES

Army Mom Strong. (2021, July 8). *Letting go of your child to the military is hard -- this can help.* Sandboxx. Retrieved November 12, 2022, from https://www.sandboxx.us/blog/letting-go-of-your-child-to-the-military-is-hard-this-can-help/

Ashraf, S. (2018, December 31). *Ultimate Travel Bucket List for 2019.* The Active Times. Retrieved November 1, 2022, from https://www.the-activetimes.com/travel/ultimate-travel-destination-bucket-list-2019/slide-3

Ashraf, S. (2019, May 22). *30 Things to Do Now That You're an Empty-Nester.* The Active Times. Retrieved November 1, 2022, from https://www.theactivetimes.com/things-to-do-for-empty-nesters/slide-23

Bailey, E. (2008, July 5). *What Happens When Anxiety Goes Untreated - Risks - Anxiety.* HealthCentral. Retrieved October 25, 2022, from https://www.healthcentral.com/article/what-happens-when-anxiety-goes-untreated

Combining Vitamin D and Omega-3s Produced the Greatest Improvements for Depression, Anxiety and Sleep. (2021, September 24). Grassroots-Health. Retrieved October 26, 2022, from https://www.grassrootshealth.net/blog/combining-vitamin-d-omega-3s-produced-greatest-improvements-depression-anxiety-sleep/

Coping With Separation And Divorce. (n.d.). Mental Health America. Retrieved November 23, 2022, from https://www.mhanational.org/separation-and-divorce

Craft, C. (2020, September 22). *6 Skills You Need to Master Before Becoming a Foster Parent.* Verywell Family. Retrieved November 9, 2022, from https://www.verywellfamily.com/skills-you-need-to-master-before-being-a-foster-parent-27075

Dillon, J. (n.d.). *Facing an Empty Nest Divorce? Watch Out for These 3 Tricky Issues.* Equitable Mediation Services. Retrieved November 23, 2022, from https://www.equitablemediation.com/blog/empty-nesters-divorce

Doyle, A. (2022, March 18). *Top 10 Best Jobs for Women Over 50.* The

Balance. Retrieved November 9, 2022, from https://www.thebalancemoney.com/best-jobs-for-women-over-50-4165332

Eagle Family. (2017, July 27). *Empty Nester Romance: How to Rekindle the Fire*. Eagle Family Ministries. Retrieved November 23, 2022, from https://www.eaglefamily.org/empty-nester-romance-rekindle-fire/

Eagle Family. (2019, July 30). *30 Fun and Flirty Date Ideas for Empty Nester Couples*. Eagle Family Ministries. Retrieved November 24, 2022, from https://www.eaglefamily.org/date-ideas-empty-nester/

Empty Nest. (2019, May 8). *How these Empty Nesters Became the Gypsy Nesters*. Empty Nest Nation. Retrieved November 1, 2022, from https://emptynestnation.com/how-these-empty-nesters-became-the-gypsy-nesters/

Emptynest. (2021, January 29). *Expert career advice for empty nesters*. Empty Nest Nation. Retrieved November 7, 2022, from https://emptynestnation.com/expert-career-advice-for-empty-nesters/

Empty Nesters: Coping With Aging Parents & College-Bound Kids. (n.d.). Friends Life Care. Retrieved November 14, 2022, from https://www.friendslifecare.org/empty-nester-aging-parents-college-bound-kids

Empty nest syndrome. (n.d.). Better Health Channel. Retrieved October 24, 2022, from https://www.betterhealth.vic.gov.au/health/healthyliving/empty-nest-syndrome#other-difficulties

Fertel, M. (n.d.). *Can I Save My Marriage with an Ultimatum?* Mort Fertel. Retrieved November 24, 2022, from https://marriagemax.com/save_my_marriage/

Fertel, M. (n.d.). *Can I Save My Marriage with an Ultimatum?* Mort Fertel. Retrieved November 24, 2022, from https://marriagemax.com/save_my_marriage/

Fertel, M. (n.d.). *How do you know if you married the right person? Did you marry the wrong person?* Mort Fertel. Retrieved November 24, 2022, from https://marriagemax.com/married-right-person/

Fertel, M. (n.d.). *How to Get Your Spouse to Change*. Mort Fertel. Retrieved November 24, 2022, from https://marriagemax.com/get-spouse-change/

Fertel, M. (n.d.). *I love you but I'm not IN LOVE with you*. Marriage Fitness with Mort Fertel. Retrieved November 24, 2022, from https://marriagemax.com/i-love-you-but-not-in-love-with-you/

Fertel, M. (n.d.). *2 Small Acts to Make a Big Difference in Your Marriage.* Marriage Fitness with Mort Fertel. Retrieved November 21, 2022, from https://marriagemax.com/2-small-acts-make-big-difference-marriage/

Foster, M. (2019, April 10). *How to Become a Foster Parent in NH: 5 Steps to Take.* Seacoast Moms. Retrieved November 9, 2022, from https://seacoast.momcollective.com/adoption-foster-care/how-to-become-a-foster-parent-in-nh-5-steps-to-take/

Garrity, A. (2019, January 11). *What Is the KonMari Method? - How to Declutter and Organize Like Marie Kondo.* Good Housekeeping. Retrieved November 28, 2022, from https://www.goodhousekeeping.com/home/organizing/a25846191/what-is-the-konmari-method/

Gish, T. (2018, August 14). *Advice for Empty Nesters on Redecorating and Remodeling a Home.* Next Avenue. Retrieved November 26, 2022, from https://www.nextavenue.org/decorating-empty-nest/

Griffiths, K. M., Crisp, D. A., Barney, L., & Reid, R. (2011, December 15). Seeking help for depression from family and friends: A qualitative analysis of perceived advantages and disadvantages. *BMC Psychiatry, 11*(196). 10.1186/1471-244X-11-196

Hausenblas, H. A., Saha, D., Dubyak, P. J., & Anton, S. D. (2013, November). Saffron (Crocus sativus L.) and major depressive disorder: a meta-analysis of randomized clinical trials. *Journal of Integrative Medicine, 11*(6), 377-383. 10.3736/jintegrmed2013056

How to Create Space in Your Relationship How to Create Space in Your Relationship. (2020, December 24). Eugene Therapy. Retrieved October 29, 2022, from https://eugenetherapy.com/article/how-to-create-space-in-your-relationship/

Hughes, M. (2011, May 17). *Scientific proof for karma? York U study finds small acts of kindness have big impact on emotional well-being | News@York.* News | York University. Retrieved November 1, 2022, from https://news.yorku.ca/2011/05/17/scientific-proof-for-karma-york-u-study-finds-small-acts-of-kindness-have-big-impact-on-emotional-well-being/

Irby, L. (2021, September 21). *A Step-by-Step Guide To Getting Out of Debt.* The Balance. Retrieved October 31, 2022, from https://www.thebalancemoney.com/steps-to-get-out-of-debt-4842113

Jackson, P. A., Froster, J., Khan, J., Pouchieu, C., Dubreuil, S., Gaudout, D., Moras, B., Pourtau, L., Joffre, F., Vaysse, C., Bertrand, K., Abrous, H., Vauzour, D., Brossaud, J., Corcuff, J. B., Capuron, L., & Kennedy, D. O. (2021, February 1). Effects of Saffron Extract Supplementation on Mood, Well-Being, and Response to a Psychosocial Stressor in Healthy Adults: A Randomized, Double-Blind, Parallel Group, Clinical Trial. *Frontiers in Nutrition.* 10.3389/fnut.2020.606124

Jane. (n.d.). *How to Declutter Your Home: Simple Step-by-Step Tips – jane at home.* jane at home. Retrieved November 26, 2022, from https://jane-athome.com/how-to-declutter-your-home

Jane. (n.d.). *How to Thrive with an Empty Nest: 33 Things to do After the Kids Leave Home.* jane at home. Retrieved November 1, 2022, from https://jane-athome.com/empty-nest-what-to-do/

Kaiser, S. (2016, May 10). *7 Keys to a Happy Relationship.* Live Happy. Retrieved November 21, 2022, from https://www.livehappy.com/relationships/7-keys-to-a-happy-relationship

Larkin, B. (2018, October 16). *40 Fun Ways to Bond with Your Adult Children — Best Life.* Best Life. Retrieved November 12, 2022, from https://bestlifeonline.com/adult-children/

Lawler, M., & Laube, J. (n.d.). *What Is Self-Care and Why Is It Critical for Your Health?* Everyday Health. Retrieved October 25, 2022, from https://www.everydayhealth.com/self-care/

Macey. (2022, June 19). *30 Unique Date Night Ideas for Empty Nesters.* The Dating Divas. Retrieved November 23, 2022, from https://www.thedatingdivas.com/30-fun-exciting-date-ideas-empty-nesters/

Mayer, B. A. (2022, September 10). *7 Workout Tips for Women Over 40.* Healthline. Retrieved November 5, 2022, from https://www.healthline.com/health/workout-tips-for-women-over-forty#take-it-easy

Mayo Clinic. (n.d.). *Depression and anxiety: Exercise eases symptoms.* Mayo Clinic. Retrieved October 26, 2022, from https://www.mayoclinic.org/diseases-conditions/depression/in-depth/depression-and-exercise/art-20046495

Mayo Clinic. (n.d.). *St. John's wort.* Mayo Clinic. Retrieved October 26, 2022, from https://www.mayoclinic.org/drugs-supplements-st-johns-wort/art-20362212

Mayo Clinic. (2022, August 3). *Support groups: Make connections, get help.* Mayo Clinic. Retrieved October 26, 2022, from https://www.mayoclinic.org/healthy-lifestyle/stress-management/in-depth/support-groups/art-20044655

Morin, A. (2020, September 16). *What Makes Some People Mentally Stronger Than Others*. Business Insider. Retrieved October 25, 2022, from https://www.businessinsider.com/what-makes-some-people-mentally-stronger-than-others-2020-9

Nicely, T. (2020, February 7). *10 Tips for Renting a Room in Your House*. Zillow. Retrieved October 31, 2022, from https://www.zillow.com/rental-manager/resources/renting-a-room-in-a-house/

Nicole. (n.d.). *10 Best Home Improvement Tips For Empty Nesters – Midlife Rambler*. Midlife Rambler. Retrieved November 4, 2022, from https://www.midliferambler.com/10-best-home-improvement-tips-empty-nesters/

Ottowa Public Health. (n.d.). *Building Social Connections - The LINK*. The Link Ottawa. Retrieved November 5, 2022, from https://www.the-linkottawa.ca/en/mental-health/building-social-connections.aspx

Parmet, S. (2016, November 18). *Fear of the unknown common to many anxiety disorders*. UIC Today. Retrieved October 25, 2022, from https://today.uic.edu/fear-of-the-unknown-common-to-many-anxiety-disorders/

Payne, J. (n.d.). *Can Menopause Cause Depression?* Johns Hopkins Medicine. Retrieved October 26, 2022, from https://www.hopkinsmedicine.org/health/wellness-and-prevention/can-menopause-cause-depression

Peregrine. (n.d.). *Empty Nest? Time for a holiday!* Peregrine Adventures. Retrieved November 1, 2022, from https://www.peregrineadventures.com/en/empty-nesters

Rabbitt, M. (2017, April 26). *Over 40? You'll Want To Do These 5 Exercises Every Week*. Prevention.com. Retrieved November 5, 2022, from https://www.prevention.com/fitness/a20449775/5-exercises-for-over-40/

Saffron Uses, Benefits & Dosage. (2022, July 29). Drugs.com. Retrieved October 26, 2022, from https://www.drugs.com/npp/saffron.html

Sawchuk, C. N. (n.d.). *Depression and anxiety: Can I have both?* Mayo Clinic. Retrieved October 25, 2022, from https://www.mayoclinic.org/diseases-conditions/depression/expert-answers/depression-and-anxiety/faq-20057989

Scott, C. (2019, October 22). *Last Child Left the Home?: Time to Plan that*

Perfect Empty Nest Party. The Healthy Voyager. Retrieved November 28, 2022, from https://healthyvoyager.com/last-child-left-the-home-time-to-plan-that-perfect-empty-nest-party

Simon, S. (2022, August 11). *Midlife Crisis: Signs And Treatments – Forbes Health*. Forbes. Retrieved October 26, 2022, from https://www.-forbes.com/health/mind/midlife-crisis/

Stern, M. (2015, March 5). *Half of Parents Say College Savings More Important Than Retirement*. Think Advisor. Retrieved October 29, 2022, from https://www.thinkadvisor.com/2015/03/05/half-of-parents-say-college-savings-more-important-than-retirement/?t=the-client

Strategies for Overcoming Empty Nest Syndrome. (n.d.). Spence Counseling Center. Retrieved October 29, 2022, from https://spencecounselingcenter.com/strategies-for-overcoming-empty-nest-syndrome/

Stress. (n.d.). Better Health Channel. Retrieved October 25, 2022, from https://www.betterhealth.vic.gov.au/health/healthyliving/stress

Suni, E. (2022, April 15). *Mental Health and Sleep*. Sleep Foundation. Retrieved October 26, 2022, from https://www.sleepfoundation.org/mental-health

Tibbetts, C. (2022, February 18). *Alone for the Holidays: Empty Nest Survival Tips*. She Buys Travel. Retrieved November 24, 2022, from https://shebuystravel.com/holiday-empty-nest-survival-tips/

Tips on Rebuilding Your Credit. (2022, January 11). Capital One. Retrieved October 31, 2022, from https://www.capitalone.-com/learn-grow/money-management/ways-rebuild-credit/?external_id=WWW_XXXXX_ZZZ_ONL-SE_ZZZZZ_T_SEM2_ZZZZ_c_Zs_63829242-5647-4935-bf94-dae757b2cfb6_601512832975_715370&target_id=kwd-131377645&gclid=Cj0KCQjwnP-ZBhDiARIsAH3FSReORs-UuVmRXf

Tjornehoj, T. (n.d.). *The Relationship Between Anxiety and Depression - Hartgrove Behavioral Health System*. Hartgrove Hospital. Retrieved October 26, 2022, from https://www.hartgrovehospital.com/relationship-anxiety-depression/

Ubaidi, B. A. (2017, September 27). Empty-Nest Syndrome: Pathway to "Construction or Destruction". *Journal of Family Medicine and Disease Prevention, 3*(3). 10.23937/2469-5793/1510064

Voll, D. (2022, June 27). *8 Career Tips For Empty Nesters Returning To*

Work. CrunchyTales. Retrieved November 7, 2022, from https://www.crunchytales.com/8-career-tips-for-empty-nesters-returning-to-work/

Weinberg, P. (2021, January 29). *Expert career advice for empty nesters*. Empty Nest Nation. Retrieved November 9, 2022, from https://emptynestnation.com/expert-career-advice-for-empty-nesters/

What is St John's wort? (2022, January). Mind. Retrieved October 26, 2022, from https://www.mind.org.uk/information-support/drugs-and-treatments/complementary-and-alternative-therapies/st-john-s-wort/

Why Side Hustles are Ideal for Empty Nesters. (2019, April 30). Empty Nest Nation. Retrieved November 9, 2022, from https://emptynestnation.com/why-side-hustles-are-ideal-for-empty-nesters/